Building Client and Business Relationships

Pilos Learning Institute © 2022

Contents

Section 1- Basic Communication in Sales 6
- Interpersonal Communication 7
- Defining Interpersonal Communication 7
- Activity One: What is Your Definition of a Skilled Communicator? 8
- Activity Two: Reflecting on Your Own Communication Skills 8
- Communication Process Elements 12
- Basic Communication in Sale 13
- Relationship Selling 15
  - Elements in the Relationship Process 16
- Building Trust and Loyalty 18
- Verbal Communication 18
  - A Positive Mindset 19
- Chapter Summary 20

Chapter Two- Nurturing Relationships 22
- Communication Styles 23
- Identifying Your Customer's Communication Style 25
  - Four Main Communication Styles 26
  - Activity: Your Dominant Communication Style Quiz 27
  - Adapting Your Style 27
- Selling to Different Communication Styles 28
- Bonus Content 30
- Non-Verbal Communication 31
  - Body Language 32
  - Reading Customer Body Language 32
  - Positive and Negative Non-Verbal Cues 33

Activity: Practicing Non-Verbal Cues and Gestures 36

Avoiding Common Negative Non-Verbal Actions 37

10 Tips for Better Sales Body Language 38

Making Eye Contact 38

The Importance of Eye Contact in Sales 39

Eye Contact during Virtual Interactions 39

Activity: Non-Verbal Cues in a Sales Meeting (Aiyana and Mr. Chang) Case Study 40

Bonus Content 45

Networking Strategies to Connect with Other Businesses 45

Practice Your Elevator Sales Pitch 45

Be an Active Chamber of Commerce Member – Attend their Events 46

Activity: Connecting with your Local Chamber of Commerce 48

Activity: Local, Regional, National Industry Associations 49

Bonus Content 51

Chapter Summary 51

Chapter 3: Enhanced Communications in Sales 53

Listening 53

Activity: Listening Self-Assessment 54

Good Listener / Bad Listener 55

Listening Process 56

The SIER Model 56

Active Listening 58

Characteristics of a Good Listener 59

How to Improve Listening Skills 59

Listening "Between the Lines" 60

- Activity: Sunrise Property Services Meets Bob's Cottage Services Case Study 60
  - When Things Go Wrong 63
  - Soliciting Feedback 63
  - Dealing with Negative Feedback 64
  - Positive Feedback 65
  - Bonus Content 66
- Resolving Problems 66
  - Strategies for Handling Complaints 67
- Written Communication 69
- Professional Sales Writing 70
  - Email Signatures and Automatic Replies 71
  - Written Sales Proposals 71
  - Creating Consistency in Written Communication 71
  - Online Communication 72
  - How to Respond to Online Reviews 73
  - Framework for Responding to Customer Feedback 73
  - Templates for Responding 75
  - Bonus Content 75
- Chapter Summary 76
- Chapter 4: Meetings and Presentations 77
- Introduction 77
  - Meetings 78
  - Sales Call Agenda 82
  - Sales Call Agenda and Checklist Template 84
- Contact Information 84

- Pre-Meeting Plan 85
- Meeting Flow Plan 85
- Post Meeting Plan 86
- Notes Area: 86
  - Activity: Preparing for a Sales Call: Template Search & Development 86
- Meeting Platforms 88
  - Features to Consider in Meeting Platforms 88
  - Follow Up After a Meeting 89
  - Follow Up After a Meeting 89
  - Following Up (Building Relationships) 90
- Presentations 90
  - Components of a Presentation 91
  - Focusing on Your Message During a Presentation 91
  - Customer Value Proposition 92
  - What to Bring to Your Sales Presentation 92
  - The Visual Presentation 93
  - When Presenting 93
  - Chapter Summary 95
- References 96

Section 1 - Basic Communication in Sales

In This section, you will gain exposure to:

- Recognize and use the elements of the interpersonal communication model
- Identify the value of the interactions related to relationship selling in B2C small businesses environment
- Apply basic sales-related verbal communication principles and strategies when interacting with customers

In this section you will be learning about interpersonal communication, the elements of the communication process, relationship selling, and verbal communication techniques.

It has often been said that the first "rule of business" is to stay in business. Businesses cannot survive without customers. Considering the continuing advancements in technology, savvy buyers have more options, more "switching power" and more influence over a business's ability to survive than ever before, especially small businesses, so how your communication skills are an integral part of staying in business.

In this global economy, potential customers have so many different options for everything and anything they could ever want. So, as a small business operation, how can you set yourselves apart from the competition?

Two words: Building Relationships. Being able to build good relationships is all about understanding basic communication and enhancing your interpersonal communication skills.

Have you ever decided to use a particular small business even though there were other options available? If so, it was most likely because of positive interpersonal skills from the business owner or their sales representatives. Very often, customers make decisions based on how confident they are made to feel about the sales interaction. When there is a loyal customer, it is most likely due to relationship building and strong communication.

The purpose of this section's lessons is to build on your communication skills to enhance your business relationships to potentially increase your sales. Becoming more efficient in sales through positive client relationships and a good reputation is the optimal goal.

Interpersonal Communication

Interpersonal communication in sales is an important part of building customer relationships, business networking and collaboration, employee satisfaction, and most importantly: business success.

When you are responsible for sales in a small business, you want to build positive customer and business relationships to ensure that positive exchanges of information occur. Understanding the elements of interpersonal communication and the importance it plays in your role in the small business / B2C environment will help you enhance the experiences with your clients and all internal and external customers and contacts.

Through a better understanding of interpersonal communication, you will enhance your communication skills, leading to better sales opportunities. You will also be more effective in building relationships, generating customer loyalty and building goodwill in your community.

Defining Interpersonal Communication

Before discussing what good interpersonal communication looks like, think about your own ideas or definitions of what that is.

Reflection and self-awareness are extremely powerful tools for continued growth and development and to enhance your confidence with building relationships in sales.

Reflection on what went well and where opportunities for improvements in your sales communication allows you to review scenarios and become a better representative for your business and for building sales-based relationships.

Self-awareness is critical for customer sales. It is a requirement for successful results. When you are aware of how your actions and behaviour can impact the outcomes of networking and sales, you can fine-tune your behaviours for success. Self-awareness aligns the impression your buyers have of you as a salesperson and your view of yourself as a salesperson. These need to match to build professional client relationships and trust.

Activity One: What is Your Definition of a Skilled Communicator?

Complete the following activity to help you reflect on your current understanding of interpersonal communications and your own communications skills.

For this activity, think about some people you know or have met you feel have strong interpersonal skills and are great at sales. In point-form, write down at least 5 – 8 traits or characteristics you feel make them good communicators and good at sales. In 1 or 2 paragraphs, describe their behaviours and what you feel makes them so good at what they do.

Activity Two: Reflecting on Your Own Communication Skills

Now that you have had some time to think about what your personal definition of what a skilled communicator is, take some time and reflect on your own communication skills by recalling some past behaviours and actions while working in sales and with clients. Communication can make or break a sale and recognizing what you do well and where you can improve in customer interactions will enhance your sales outcomes.

Reflection

Use the question prompts below to reflect on your own communication skills. Since self-awareness and reflection can be difficult, it is recommended that after you have provided at least 2 responses per question, talk to peers, family members or anyone you are comfortable with to see if their views align with yours and where there may be some opportunities to improve your skills as a communicator that will help you with your future sales.

Think of a time when you were at your best as a communicator.

1. What were some of your actions and behaviours?
2. Why was it a successful communication?

Think of a time when communication **did not go well** in the past.

1. What happened, or what went wrong?
2. What were some of your actions that interfered with an effective communication?

As this is a personal reflection, there are no right or wrong answers. Take some time to reflect on being more aware of the actions and behaviours that worked well for you when communicating with others and focus on building these into all of your communications to enhance your relationship building skills.

When things went well, it was a successful communication.

When things did not go well or as expected, it could have been the result of one or a combination of common factors. Some of these factors are distractions, poor listening, misunderstandings between you and the other person, not being prepared for the communication, unprofessional responses, choice of words and actions, mood and internal detractors and attitude.

Communication is a process that requires you to be fully present, prepared and to eliminate detractors. These and others are "noise" factors you will continue to learn about during relationship building. The good news is, the more you learn about them, the easier it will be to use the tools to build relationships.

Now that you have taken some time to reflect, as well as your definition of a skilled communicator and your own past experiences during sales-related interactions, can you think of any areas for improvement? Does your definition of a good communicator align with your current skills or actions?

Let's now look at that definition. Interpersonal Communication is defined as a transmission of a message between two or more people. It is a process of exchanging information through verbal and non-verbal means with feedback.

In a context of sales, interpersonal communication is a continual cycle between the salesperson and the client throughout the sales process and has the following characteristics in B2C sales:

- Each person in the communication brings varying perceptions and experiences to the process

- The message is meant to be understood
- Communicating must occur in any and all B2C sales
- You have to make decisions on how you will be communicating

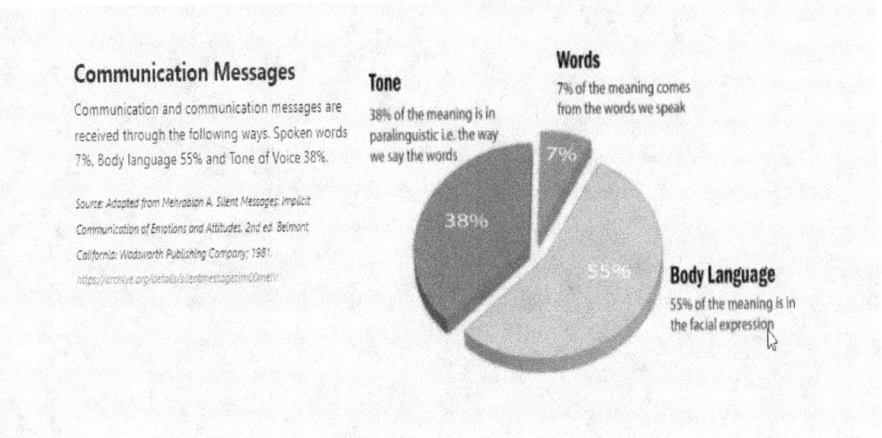

What does this tell us and why is this important to know before we work through the elements of the Interpersonal Communication model?

It tells us that how we send and receive messages is more important than what we say to clients, although it is the combination all our words, actions and behaviours that create the entire massage for our clients.

Think of the communication experience from the client's perspective. Strong communication messages and your ability to deliver them are required for successful sales outcomes.

Source: What is Customer Experience (2019) Bordeaux, J. Hubspot Blog, retrieved from https://blog.hubspot.com/service/what-is-customer-experience

Communication Process Elements

Building relationships through effective communication with clients, partners, vendors, and networking opportunities is critical to small business success. Although different approaches of positive communication need to happen with all stakeholders, there are elements of interpersonal communication that come into practise during each of these interactions.

Effective communication as a process using a variety of elements working together towards the desired end result of building relationships for sales.

Each communication process element is equally important and works together as a system. If you remove any of these elements, you will most likely experience a service failure, relationship breakdown or, if confusion or frustration occurs, it may result in not closing the sale.

Basic Communication in Sale

Element of Interpersonal	Impact on Building Relationships in Sales
Environment is the location or external environment where the communication occurs. This can be the office, store, group or individual	• Where you send or receive the message and affects the outcome of effectiveness. • Selecting the right environment for customer communication can positively enhance the outcome.
The **sender** is the initiator, the source of the interpersonal communication. This is one of the two primary elements of two-way conversation. They select a channel and	• As the sender it is important to consider the message you want your client (receiver) to get and the best way to communicate it (channel). • The role of the sender rotates between salesperson and client dependent on the stage of the communication cycle.
The **receiver** is the recipient of the communication. In a conversation, two people exchange the role of the sender and the	• You must effectively listen in order to interpret effectively and comprehend what the customer said. • You may begin the conversation in either role as the sender or receiver. Once you offer feedback to the customer, your role

The **message** is the idea, content or concept that you wish to convey to your client. Actual content of the communication itself. It's the idea the sender wants to communicate to the

The **channel** is the method in which the message is sent from the sender to the receiver. This is the transmission medium. Some examples are in person meeting.

The **encoding** is when you put the message you want to send to the client into a way, they will best understand it. (Language, gestures

The **decoding** is when your client assigns meaning through your message by converting based on their personal filters (background,

- Messages can get lost in the delivery if the chosen words or non- verbal actions or behaviours you are presenting are not understood as intended by the customer.
- The customer interprets the message based on their past experience and personal factors.
- In order to prevent service breakdowns in sales the clients' filters and how they analyze

- Face to face is the most effective channel with customers as it allows for information richness, meaning customers can hear words, tone, inflections in the voice and see your non-verbal behaviours.
- Written communication leaves room for interpretation from the client and can

- The goal is to have your client successfully decode your message to lead to understanding. If that does not occur, the result could be confusion or frustration.

- If the customer converts the message the way it was intended, the result is a successful message received.
- If it was not received the way you initially intended, service breakdowns can occur.

Feedback is the information the sender gets from the receiver in response to the message. It can be non-verbal, such as a head nod indicating understanding or it can be verbal when the receiver says, "Can you please

- Crucial element of the interpersonal communication in sales.
- Without feedback you have a monologue.
- Feedback is very important in determining if the communication was effective or if we need to repeat or change the message to be sure it is correctly understood.

Noise is physiological factors that interfere with the accurate reception of information in the communication and

- Refers to anything that interferes or disrupts the communication process.
- This can be psychological factors such as emotional condition, mood, level of attention
- This can include environmental factors such as sounds, interruptions, barriers.

Filters is anything that can distort or impact the message being received. Anything that impacts how someone will process and

- Filters can include attitudes, biases, past experiences, education, beliefs and values, culture, gender, background, etc.
- These can impact our client judgement and perception of the message being received.

Building on the foundation of interpersonal communications and the communication process in general, we will now focus on relationship selling, which is all about creating rapport with your clients and building loyalty.

Relationship Selling

Relationship selling, similar to consultive selling is all about the connection and relationship between a salesperson and their customers and/or prospective buyers. While details about the product or service and pricing are important, the focus and priority in relationship selling is on the interaction and the trust being built between the salesperson and the customer.

Through relationship selling, salespeople become consultants (consultive sales), partners, collaborators and problem solvers for the customer. The mutually beneficial goal is to build long-term relationships, trust and loyalty.

Elements in the Relationship Process

There are four main elements in the relationship process used by salespeople to build relationships. (1) Analyze customers' needs – a salesperson cannot prospect effectively unless they anticipate, uncover and analyze the customer's needs (consultive role), (2) Recommend a solution and gain commitment for the purchase (trust), (3) Implement the recommendation (as partner, collaborator, problem solver), and (4) Maintain and grow the relationship (loyalty). (Futrell & Valvasori, 2015)

Creating a Good First Impression

To build relationships, you must first make a good first impression.

Without that positive first impression, you will face extra barriers to creating trust and building loyalty with potential customers. It is critical to small business success that you take advantage of that opportunity to begin building trust through effective communication with not only clients, but with business partners, vendors, and networking connections. You want to get their attention for the right reasons. Although different approaches work with different customers based on their consumer characteristics and communication styles, here a few tips on what you need to consider to be able to continue the conversation and to build trust and customer loyalty.

FIRST IMPRESSIONS

Have a "winning" smile
(smile with your eyes and your voice!)

Present yourself appropriately
(dress for the occasion)

Be genuine — be yourself

Be open and confident

Be positive

Be on time. Respect clients time

Be courteous and attentive

Use "small talk" when appropriate
(polite conversation about
unimportant matters like the
weather, plans for the day, etc.)

When meeting people, 7% of
what our potential client's
impression of us is through
spoken words, body language
55% and tone of voice 33%.

Creating that positive first impression opens opportunities for you to continue to create trust and build loyalty with customers.

You will continue to learn about building trust through effective communication in an effort to create a loyal customer.

Adapted from: Source: *Making a Great First Impression.* (n.d). Mind Tools. Retrieved from:
https://www.mindtools.com/CommSkll/FirstImpressions.htm.

Building Trust and Loyalty

Relationship selling creates customer loyalty by paying continuous attention to building relationships with customers. Small businesses need to take the time required to build the trust and must understand that the long-term value of a loyal customer is all about the interaction with the client, not the transaction. When trust has been built in a relationship, other offers from your competition become less important to that loyal customer.

The best part of building relationships in small businesses is that once it has been built, a loyal customer may become a salesperson for you and your business out in the community, to their friends and their families.

That is the goal of a small business, positive word-of-mouth and the power that it holds. This happens through building relationships, the basis of relationship selling. There is a saying that people do not care how much you know, until they know how much you care.

The best salespeople are those that are great at building relationships. How do people build relationships? They make it about the customer they are working with and not about the sale or themselves. These relationships start with a sincere interest in the people, not about the sale. Sales often follow the relationship, whether it is the person you have built a relationship with, or someone that trusts them when they mention you as a trustworthy option.

Verbal Communication

Verbal communication consists of the words we say, as well as the tone and the pitch we use, when speaking. It is how we make connections with others, and how we give and receive information. Verbal communication, as well as non-verbal communication in sales occur during face-to-face communication, over the telephone and in virtual meetings and connections. The words you use in selling not only communicate information about your products or services, they also communicate powerful messages about you as salesperson and the company you represent.

A Positive Mindset

The Little Things

"Little Things Matter," is the name of a blog that was created by entrepreneur Todd Smith. Included below are his 10 (plus one) suggestions about verbal communication skills that he believes are worth mastering in both our personal and professional lives. It is a simple way to demonstrate the importance that verbal communication holds in small business sales.

1. Be Friendly- People who communicate with a friendly professional tone and a warm smile almost always have the edge. Why? Consumers are drawn to people who make them feel good.
2. Think Before You Speak- The blog article cites a clever proverb to illustrate the key to developing this skill: "It is better to remain silent and be thought a fool, than to open your mouth and remove all doubt!" No doubt — can't argue with that!

Be Clear

When you have something to say, ask yourself, "What is the clearest way I may communicate this point?" Nothing else to add here, I think that was clear.

- Don't Talk Too Much
- The more YOU talk — the LESS you LISTEN to what others are saying.
- Be Your Authentic Self

People are attracted to people who speak from the heart — people who are genuine, transparent and real. This helps build trust in relationships and humanizes the experience for clients.

Practice Humility

Be humble. Todd says it is one of the most attractive qualities you may possess — and one of the most significant predictors of someone who is capable of capturing the respect of others.

- Speak With Confidence

- This skill may seem to compete with that of practicing humility, but important to remember that this is confidence without sacrificing modesty.
- Focus on Your Body

As we will continue to learn in future modules, body language plays a significant role in communication and our clients interpreting the message.

Be Concise

The author recommends that we constantly ask ourselves, "How may I say what needs to be said with the fewest number of words possible — while still being courteous and respectful?" An important piece of sales is getting the biggest impact of your spoken words with your customers to make the sale.

Learn the Art of Listening

Show a sincere interest in what is being said. Stay in the moment with the client; ask thoughtful relevant questions and listen for the messages from the customer to help with their needs. Avoid interrupting. Listening is an essential element of communicating effectively. As Celeste Headlee mentions in her Ted Talk below, "no one has ever listened their way out of a job".

The Plus One: Verbal Modelling (or Mirroring)

Tip- people are more attracted to those similar to themselves and that we can use this in sales to our advantage to build relationships through the practise of verbal modelling (or mirroring). When we match the tone and modulation of the speaker, we become more likeable and that makes our communication more effective!

Source: 10 Verbal Communication Skills Worth Mastering. (n.d). Smith, T. Little Things Matter. Retrieved from: https://www.littlethingsmatter.com/blog/2010/11/30/10-verbal-communication-skills-worth-mastering/

Chapter Summary

In this chapter: Basic Communication in Sales you have learned about the communication process, interpersonal communication elements and consumer characteristics that will help you enhance your relationship selling skills and verbal communication techniques. You were also introduced to a variety of great speakers offering tips to support your learning in the context of building sales related relationships in small business B2C environments. Think about how you can use these new skills in your everyday sales practice.

Chapter Two- Nurturing Relationships

In this chapter you will be learning about communication styles and non-verbal communication techniques that can either positively or negatively impact your sales strategies. You will also learn about partnership and networking strategies to help you connect with other businesses.

Nurturing relationships is critical in today's sales environment. Taking time to understand your clients and to maintain relationships over time helps build brand loyalty and trust. If you nurture and build those relationships into genuine connections it can result in mutually beneficial long-term relationships which lead to more sales for your business.

Sales success is not only about one sale, it's also about the potential and future sales that your customers or partners, or other businesses may be connected with. Regardless of your products or services, you are in the business of people, especially in a B2C sales environment. Nurturing relationships matter.

Nurturing relationships can occur face-to-face, or virtually, through video, telephone or through social media platforms. In small business, relationships matter more than ever considering the continuing advancements in technology, savvy buyers, and more options available for customers.

Applying customer-focused sales approaches, having solid product knowledge and viable sales solutions all help build customer loyalty. A loyal customer adds long term value to you in sales due to the fact that they return to do business with you again and again. Repeat business is a testament to the relationship that the client has with your products and services, and with you. It is much more time-consuming and costly to find new customers than it is to invest in creating loyal customers through nurtured relationships. The concept of nurturing relationships becomes a critical business decision.

Communication Styles

We all have behaviours that repeat, and those that others are able to observe in our actions, voice, eye movement, expression, and posture. These are referred to as behaviour, social or communication styles.

Understanding these varying styles will help you with adaptive selling which is the altering of your behaviour in the sales process to improve your communication with your customer. This requires some rapid adjustments of your behaviours to collect information regarding the customers' needs so you can maximize your response to your potential customer.

Being aware of your style and how you can adapt towards the customer is a way that can help build rapport and nurture the relationship for the sale. Here are a few things about communication styles that will help you understand it in the context of sales.

COMMUNICATION *Style* FACTORS

Individuals all have their own style – everyone communicates in a different way

No one style is better than the other or the right style, they are just different ways of thinking and behaving

Understanding how to adapt and apply the right style to each situation in business to consumer sales is critical for success

Understanding consumer styles and your own self-awareness allows you to be flexible in the sales experience for your clients and to adapt to their style to be in their comfort zone

Each client is unique in their overall style with some dominant traits presenting in the sales interaction that can give us clues to how we can mirror or reflect their behaviours while selling

Communication styles are based on two main factors of behavior: Dominance and Sociability.

Although these are some guidelines to help you with your sales techniques and develop strong long lasting relationships with your networks and clients, these are just guidelines. Each relationship you develop is unique and requires you to approach everyone as an individual as you gather more information through trust and nurturing the relationship.

Identifying Your Customer's Communication Style

There are four main communication styles, one of which presents as a dominant style within each person. Understanding your customer's communication style through some of their dominant behaviours gives you an advantage when you are selling to them. There are a variety of names for each style, some are referred to with titles or as colors or as animals according on a number of theorists.

Below is a summary of four communication styles, referred to with titles and as colors. It is important to remember that none of these styles are better than the other, they are just different, just as your sales rapport strategy should be for each customer.

Four Main Communication Styles

Driver (Red) (action focus): the person who takes charge and wants solutions. • Goal orientated • Needs to see results • Quick reaction time, decisive • Independent • Practical • Direct • Controlled facial expressions • High Dominance • Low Sociability 	**Analytical (Blue)** (process focus): the person who values accuracy and details. • Fact orientated • Needs to be accurate • Organized, systematic • Slow reaction time • Serious, industrious • Methodical, tenacious • Low Dominance • Low Sociability
Amiable/Personal (Green) (people focus): the person who prioritizes relationships. • Personal security, acceptance • Cooperative • Personable • Enthusiastic, loyal • Perceptive • Hates conflict • Prefers to work in teams • High Sociability • Low Dominance 	**Expressive/Intuitive (Yellow)** (idea focus): the idea person. • Sociable • Enthusiastic, impulsive • Future orientated • Conceptual, innovative • Egotistical • Needs to be accepted by others • Undisciplined • High Sociability • High Dominance

As we have just seen, everyone communicates differently, and self-awareness is an important step in becoming better at building relationships. There are a lot of quizzes online to help you identify your dominant style, and a lot of theories and research on the different styles. If you are interested in researching this idea further, you will note that they typically qualify into four main categories and although they may have different titles, they are all very similar.

As someone in the business of selling, it may be valuable to you to dig a bit deeper into each of these areas to help you with your ability to build relationships.

Activity: Your Dominant Communication Style Quiz

The following activity will help you improve your interactions with all communication styles.

Take the time to consider the questions and learn a bit more about yourself so you can interact better with others during your sales calls and meetings.

If, for example, you are a style that tends to be fast paced and working with a potential customer who has a slower paced style, you will need to "flex" or adapt your style to maximize their comfort level.

Also, being aware that sometimes your communication style will have both advantages and frustrations for others. Acknowledging these frustrations can help you remove your blind spots, help you as a salesperson and make you better at building relationships.

Follow the link below to the website for a free Communication Style quiz.

Take your time and consider the questions to learn a little more about yourself so you can interact better with others.

Note that everyone is a mix of each style, with one dominant.

When you finish the quiz, a short synopsis on your style will be generated for you.

IMPORTANT: If you want to access this later, save it or print it, because if you don't, it will disappear when you leave the page.

https://www.keela.co/communications-style-quiz

Adapting Your Style

A big part of improving your communication skills is being able to adapt your style. Here are pointers on why adapting your style is critical to you in sales, an important part of adaptive selling.

- Be very attentive and know who you are before you can help others.
- Be able to flex (adapt) your style to develop rapport and build relationships with people from each quadrant in sales. If you do not flex, you risk getting sales and will not be successful.

- Style flexing is a sales strategy that can be learned to help you make a connection and is an adaption of your style to accommodate the needs of your customer.
- Adapting your style adds value to the sales process. People want to do business with those they can relate to and feel comfortable with, potentially increasing your sales.

Selling to Different Communication Styles

If you treat all your customers the same during sales call, you most likely find yourself frustrated during or after sales calls. In sales, to build the best relationships, you realize that everyone behaviour is not the same and so your interactions should also be personalized to their different communication styles. People behave differently and you must understand where they come from and how they communicate to build the best sales relationship.

These tips below will help you understand the different communication styles you'll experience on sales calls. It will give you practical tips on how to adapt your communication to different communication styles. If you can cater your selling style to the person that you're selling to, you'll see positive improvements in your sales results. There are 4 main communication styles: Drivers, Analytical, Amiable and Expressive. These styles can be found everywhere in all markets, some styles are more dominant in specific industries based on the nature of the business.

Driver (Red) (action focus):	Analytical/Inquisitive (Blue) (process focus):
<ul><li>The person who takes charge and wants solutions.</li><li>Potential prospect driven by the bottom line.</li><li>Get to the point quickly.</li><li>Communicate to this customer how they benefit from your product or service.</li><li>Be clear and direct.</li><li>Align with their goals.</li><li>High Dominance</li><li>Low Sociability</li></ul>	<ul><li>Organized and systematic</li><li>The person who values accuracy and details.</li><li>Requires a lot of data and information to make decisions.</li><li>Needs time and space to review the data</li><li>Put a lot of time and energy into thinking things through</li><li>Be sure to follow up with this customer on the date scheduled.</li><li>Does not like to be wrong</li></ul>
Amiable/Rational (Green) (people focus):	**Expressive/Intuitive (Yellow)** (idea focus):
<ul><li>People that prioritize relationships.</li><li>Value making a connection</li><li>Value personal security and acceptance.</li><li>Offer a cooperative approach.</li><li>Want to make everyone happy and comfortable</li><li>Considerate</li><li>Intentional</li><li>Can be hard to gauge real thoughts and opinions.</li><li>High Sociability</li><li>Low Dominance</li></ul>	<ul><li>The idea person.</li><li>They want to relate with you</li><li>Story tellers</li><li>Share their life story</li><li>Very personable with professionalism.</li><li>Lots of gestures and facial expressions</li><li>Not very interested in the details</li><li>Want to know the bigger picture</li><li>Very Sociable</li><li>High Sociability</li><li>High Dominance</li></ul>

The ability to identify your customer's communication style quickly helps you respond in the most impactful and effective way to build trust in that relationship. It is really important that you understand the styles to best sell to each style. It is also important to note, that although there are four core communication styles, some people are harder to determine their style as they approach scenarios with a variation of styles based on how they flex or adapt based on circumstances. Below are some tips on how to best respond to the four core styles: Driver, Analytical, Amiable and Expressive.

Driver (Red) (action focus):	Analytical/Inquisitive (Blue) (process focus):
<ul><li>Get to the point quickly.</li><li>Communicate to this customer how they benefit from your product or service.</li><li>Be clear and direct.</li><li>You cannot use too much pressure as they want to be in control. Provide them the control desired.</li><li>Be sure to show drivers the reason why</li><li>You will want to use words that are reflective of their tendencies such as. "This is going to be very quick", "Can you tell me real fast about...."</li><li>Align with their goals.</li></ul>	Provide as much information needed to help them make a decision. You need to pace the conversation and then take the lead. You will want to reflect on their identify as a detailed person Offer space for the client to review the information provided, work the numbers. Be sure to follow up with this customer on the date scheduled. Organized, systematic <ul><li>Low Dominance</li><li>Low Sociability</li></ul>
Amiable/Rational (Green) (people focus):	Expressive/Intuitive (Yellow) (idea focus):
<ul><li>Make a connection with them as they value personal security and acceptance.</li><li>Offer a cooperative approach.</li><li>Try to gain a commitment of the sale or a follow up meeting to ensure you are making progress as this style is hard to gauge the outcome.</li><li>Add a little pressure as often will not make a decision unless there is some.</li><li>Be perceptive of their needs and take control of the conversation in a sensitive way.</li><li>Ask them open ended questions and give them time to respond.</li><li>Acknowledge differing ideas or thoughts and address them in a non-accusatory way to gain insight to their needs.</li></ul>	<ul><li>Be personable with professionalism.</li><li>Steer the customer where you need the sales conversation to go as they are very sociable.</li><li>Do not try to take control of the conversation but redirect it as needed.</li><li>Discuss future benefits and big picture.</li><li>You will want to minimize their ability to get distracted in a story by framing questions carefully. "What are your top priorities for the product"</li><li>Frame questions to get short responses</li><li>Ask closed ended questions to get a specific answer</li><li>Ask data based questions to extract the information you need for the sale.</li></ul>

Bonus Content

If you have a further interest in topics related to communication styles, take the time to visit some of the self-assessment surveys, available online. Select the links to visit these well-known commercial assessments to help further your understanding of your communication style. These are tools that can be used to learn more about yourself and be better equipped to interact with customers in sales.

- Insights: https://www.thecolourworks.com/insights-discovery-colour-types-guide/

- DISC: https://www.discprofile.com/what-is-disc
- Myers-Briggs Type Indicator: https://www.myersbriggs.org/my-mbti-personality-type/mbti-basics/

Non-Verbal Communication

A big part of communication is something called non-verbal communication. Non-verbal communication consists of the unspoken messages that people send as cues through gestures, body positioning, movements, facial expressions, vocal qualities, and pauses. Non-verbal communication in sales occurs during face to face communication, in virtual meetings and connections and even over the telephone.

These non-verbal messages are often sent in combination with verbal communication. The non-verbal messages you use in selling not only communicate information, they also communicate powerful messages about you as salesperson and the company you represent.

To be successful in sales and networking, the awareness that you are constantly sending non-verbal messages is required. This awareness will optimize each client encounter. It is important for you to remember that your non-verbal actions and behaviours are more powerful than your words and they could override the message to your client.

When customers are uncertain about the meaning of the verbal communication, they tend to focus on the non-verbal messaging of your gestures and movements for clarification.

Non-verbal communication techniques apply to face-to-face and virtual interactions. Factors such as communication style, demographics, past experiences, culture, geography and many other factors can result in misinterpretation from clients.

Body Language

The non-verbal signals you use to communicate your feelings and intentions are also referred to as body language. They include posture, facial expressions, tone of voice, eye contact, body positioning, hand gestures and more.

Body language is that non-verbal communication that we all do – often done instinctively or sub-consciously rather than deliberately. But whether you are aware of it or not, you are sending strong messages that may be positive or negative. They can either put people at ease, and build trust or they can offend and confuse, ultimately undermining your actual intentions.

Your ability to recognize and interpret body language will help you pick up on issues or emotions in others, as well as yourself.

Reading Customer Body Language

Great sales people pay attention to all body language signals from prospects and customers. How a prospect or customer uses gestures, positions their body, moves, alters the qualities of their voice and/or their facial expressions are all messages being sent to you.

Gestures are the use of body parts such as the hands, arms, head and shoulders to enhance the communication. These non-verbal gestures can add emotion to the communication.

Facial expressions are about all the emotions that can be communicated through the position or movements of the facial muscles. All these motions convey the emotional state of the customer or, for that matter, you, as the sales agent.

Vocal qualities are the sounds or inflection of the voice used to send a message. These attributes to verbal communication send non-verbal messages between you and your customers. These include pitch, volume, pace, pronunciation and quality.

Through careful observation, you can become an expert at reading body language. The more you observe the indicators reviewed in the module, the better you will become.

Positive and Negative Non-Verbal Cues

Interpreting messages from your customer's non-verbal cues and behaviours helps you better diagnose their needs. Aligning your message and non-verbal cues can help your customers quickly feel comfortable around you. Projecting positive non-verbal cues will enhance the selling experience.

To communicate more effectively, it is important to build your awareness of non-verbal cues so that you can identify and appropriately react to your customer's positive and negative body language and exhibiting your own positive cues. Here are some positive and negative examples of non-verbal cues.

Non-verbal Cue	Importance in Sales	Positive Examples	Negative Examples
Facial Expressions: One or more positions or movements of the placement of muscles on the face. These motions convey the emotional state of a customer or sales agent to the other.	Keep your facial expressions calm and relaxed when communicating with your prospects and clients. This allows them to feel relaxed and build trust.	• Smiling • Raising Eyebrows • Relaxed Mouth	• Furrowing your eyebrow • Scrunching up your nose • Rolling your eyes • Wrinkling your forehead
Gestures: The use of body parts such as the hands, arms, head and shoulders to enhance the communication. These non-verbal gestures can add emotion to the communication. These motions convey the emotional state of a customer or sales agent to the other.	Gestures in sales can help to gain and maintain attention, clarify or deepen the description. Open flowing gestures help explain messages to the customers as you build rapport. The key to building trust and loyalty is to be seemingly natural. In sales you should align your gestures with verbal without distracting the customer and you should feel relaxed.	• Open arms • Palms open and upward • Nodding affirmatively • Leaving your torso and body barrier free	• Closed arms • Dismissive hand gestures • Restrained movements • Tightly crossed arms • Hands in pockets • Hands or fingers intertwined • Pointing finger or object at customer • Subdued or minimal hand gestures
Eye Contact: Occurs when two people look at each other's eyes at the same time. It is key component of non-verbal communication	Eye contact tells your customer that you are attuned to them and can lead to a deeper relationship. Good eye contact can build trust and help you read your customers The typical period of time to hold eye contact is between 5 to 10 seconds with an occasional glance away.	• Looking back and forth between your products or sales material within the 5 to 10 second range. • Eyes wide open	• Avoiding eye contact with your customer • Looking down before answering questions. • Maintaining eye contact for too long can seem aggressive or rude • Looking away from customer and outside of the sales area • Blinking excessively

Non-verbal Cue	Importance in Sales	Positive Examples	Negative Examples
Posture/Position: Your body positioning or stance	Exhibiting a strong and straight stance of confidence with open body language you appear ready to assist your customers in sales	• Walk tall and confidently • Leaning forward when your customer is speaking • Observing personal space	• Slouching • Standing with slumped shoulders • Shuffling or dragging your feet • Arms as barriers across your body • Positioning too close • Turning away from customer
Vocal Cues: Sounds or inflection of the voice used to send a message. Attributes to verbal communication that send non-verbal messages to the customer. These include pitch, volume, pace, pronunciation and quality.	Vocal cues in sales have the ability to weaken the message or make it stronger. For example if you tell a customer you "Appreciate their business" but have an angry tone, the message is confusing and weakens the message. This type of confusion impacts trust in the relationship.	• Select right volume of voice while speaking. • Change in tone compliments the story • Use vocal variety and punctuation • Speak at approximately 125 to 150 words per minute • Allow pauses for processing	• Speaking too quietly or too loudly for the environment • Monotone when speaking • Raising inflection inappropriately • Not providing time for a thoughtful response in the conversation
Appearance and Grooming: The way you present yourself physically through the areas of cleanliness, wardrobe and attitude.	Proper appearance in sales sends the customers a message about you and contributes to their first impression on your level of trust and professionalism. Opinions are typically made in less than 30 seconds.	• Does not need to be designer or expensive but it should be well maintained and clean • Formality should match the environment. • Well-fitting clothes	• Big bulky or too much jewelry • Wrinkled, stained or damaged clothing • Formality of clothes does not match environment – too formal or too informal for event or location

Non-verbal Cue	Importance in Sales	Positive Examples	Negative Examples
Spatial Cues: Nonverbal messages sent based on how close or far someone stands from others	The distance or zones where during your sales interactions make people feel most comfortable. This varies in each culture and with each person but the best range or distance for social and work is between 4 and 12 feet.	Distance Defined: • Intimate (0-18 in) • Personal (18in to 4 ft) • Social and work (4-12ft) • Public (12 ft or more)	• When you get inside a client's comfort zone, they will likely move away, become anxious possibly defensive or offended

Activity: Practicing Non-Verbal Cues and Gestures

Communicating the message, you intend to send is critical to build trust in relationships and attract new business. This activity is an opportunity to practice and identify gaps between your intentions and reality of the message being communicated through body language, gestures, body positioning, vocal qualities, facial expressions and timing. Take some time to work through practicing nonverbal cues and gestures below.

Review the list of emotions below.

Select 4 and videotape yourself as you practice expressing non-verbal cues that demonstrate those 4 emotions.

- Happiness
- Disgust
- Sadness
- Excitement
- Surprise
- Anger
- Contentment
- Concern
- Fear
- Frustration

Note: Optionally, you may also want to practice in front of an observer you know and trust to give you feedback before you videotape yourself.

Demonstrate all aspects of non-verbal communication and body language, like gestures, body positioning and movements (arms, hands, shoulders and head), vocal qualities, facial expressions, pauses, etc.

Call out each chosen emotion before expressing them and try to imagine yourself in a sales scenario with a customer as you express the emotions.

After you have videotaped your emotions, review each attempt to get a good sense of what your non-verbal cues may look like to others during your interpersonal communications.

As you review and analyze each attempt, answer the following questions:

1. Did your emotions come through on the video as you had intended?
2. Did the message you were trying to send appear as you had intended?
3. If there were differences, why was that the case?
4. What could the impact be on your sales and networking interactions?

Communicating the message, you intend to send is critical to build trust in relationships and attract new business. Identifying through practice if there is gaps between your intentions and reality of the message being communicated will help you eliminate any confusion.

Avoiding Common Negative Non-Verbal Actions

The following are some common negative non-verbal actions that could cause your client relationships to breakdown. You work so hard to build trust and nurture your relationships, try to avoid these common negative behaviours.

1. Looking at your phone while talking with someone: Put the phone away and out of sight when you are on a site visit, in a meeting or networking. When you are looking at your phone, you are missing opportunities to connect or sending a message that you are not interested in those around you or what they are saying.
2. Unprofessional handshakes: In client relationships greeting with a firm handshake (palm to palm) followed by a few firm not tight pumps up and down can lead to a positive impression. Avoid a loose or tight grip.

3. Pointing a finger or other objects: Pointing comes across as an aggressive gesture. If you are directing a client do so with your palm open and up. If you can take some steps with them in the direction you wanted them to look or go.
4. Crossing your arms: Placing anything between you and the client is a barrier to communication. It sends a message of closed off or opposition. Keep the space between you and the client. Be sure they are positioned between your shoulders with your chest facing them to demonstrate you are open to learning more about them or their business challenges.
5. Raising your eyebrows: This action indicates you are skeptical or disbelief of what is being said.
6. Fidgeting: You want to come across as focused and interested. When you chew your nails or bite your lip, tap surfaces, twirl your hair or sway back and forth you appear annoyed or anxious.

10 Tips for Better Sales Body Language

- Smile
- Mirror the other person
- Watch your space between you and the customer
- Lean in and face towards them in your conversation
- Make eye contact
- Speak at a professional pace
- Stand tall and straight
- Align your verbal and non-verbal messaging
- Keep your torso open and barrier free
- Confirm your perceptions

Making Eye Contact

There is a saying that "our eyes are the windows to our soul". There is a lot of power and meaning in effective eye contact. Eyes are used to communicate and they reflect comfort level and sincerity. When you are speaking with a client in-person, making eye contact is critical.

The Importance of Eye Contact in Sales

Why is good eye contact so important in sales? Eye contact tells your customer that you are attuned to them. It can also lead to a deeper relationship. Good eye contact can build trust and help you read your customers better. The typical period of time to hold eye contact is between 5 to 10 seconds with an occasional glance away.

It indicates that communication has gone well and customers feel cared for when done correctly. Maintaining eye contact for too long can seem aggressive or rude. Making eye contact with a customer while exhibiting negative non-verbal cues such as scrunched up facial features, highly raised eyebrows will have the opposite effect desired.

This is equally true during virtual communications. When you are on video, your eye contact sends non-verbal messages. Keeping eye contact means that you are interested in sending a message to your client that you care about them.

Eye Contact during Virtual Interactions

Always do whatever you can to keep contact with the camera during any virtual interactions. Try not to look at the other people in the call when someone is speaking. Exhibit the behaviour you would want to see if you were at an in-person meeting. If someone is speaking, that should be the person you are making virtual eye contact with so you can monitor their non-verbal cues. Try to stay close (but not too close) to your camera location, this allows easier access to look directly into the camera. It is also recommended to put your speaking notes right beside your camera.

How to Make Eye Contact on a Video Call Video Takeaway: The strongest temptation on a virtual sales call is to look at the person you are speaking with screen picture or video. Often the camera is in an alternate location then the image on the screen. Look at the camera and maintain eye contact with it as awkward as it may feel. It is ok to take glances at the images of the people you are speaking but return to the camera. Another tip offered was to change the view, position or layout of the speaker to place them as close to your camera as possible.

Activity: Non-Verbal Cues in a Sales Meeting (Aiyana and Mr. Chang) Case Study

Take some time to review this case study of Sunrise Landscaping where sales representative Aiyana visits a customer in their community. It is her first face to face sales call with Sunrise and where she makes a first impression through her nonverbal actions and behaviours. Non-verbal communication consists of the unspoken messages that people send as cues through gestures, body positioning, movements, facial expressions, vocal qualities, and pauses. The case study is an opportunity to identify the positive and negative nonverbal actions demonstrated during the sales call.

Note that the Sunrise Property Services Case Study Background information is available if you would like to re-read it before starting this activity.

As you read through the following Case Study, note all of the non-verbal cues between Aiyana and Mr. Chang. Identify which of these cues you would consider positive and which ones you would consider to be negative. Also note if and how any of the negative non-verbal cues could have been prevented.

Put yourself in Aiyana's shoes and reflect on her sales/site visit. After you have read through the Case Study and have noted the positive and negative non-verbal cues, you can select "Feedback" to reveal them as highlighted in Green for positive and in Red for negative cues.

As you go through the activity, think about the following:

Each non-verbal cue is important and works together as a message to and from your customers. If you are unaware of negative body language cues, you will most likely experience a service failure, relationship breakdown or unintended messaging to your clients.

By identifying opportunities for improvements through the non-verbal cues Aiyana was sending and receiving throughout the sales visit, you can improve your own sales-based relationship building skills and become a better representative of your business.

Aiyana, Sunrise Property Services' newest team member is responsible for sales and growth of the landscaping side of the business and had a busy day scheduled.

Aiyana had four in-person sales meetings scheduled: 2 residential customers (both at cottage locations) and 2 local businesses, (a marina and restaurant on the water).

From the office manager's notes, all appeared to be large jobs. This was her first day of actual sales and site visits since she has been building her prospects list through social media, telephone and virtual meetings.

Aiyana noted that the office manager planned the timing of the visits based on their locations to maximize her time with the customers.

She was dressed for success in her power suit and favourite heels and was a 15 minute drive away from her first appointment with the Muskoka Marina to discuss building a garden retaining wall around their public docking area. The office manager also noted a meeting confirmation from the day before, so to her knowledge, they were expecting her.

Aiyana arrived 10 minutes before the scheduled meeting, noted the beautiful property and read her notes again. She was meeting Eric Chang, long-time owner of the marina. She fixed her hair, touched up her makeup and headed towards the main entrance.

She was greeted upon her entrance by a smiling, friendly marina team member.

"Good morning, I am Aiyana with Sunrise Property Services here to meet Mr. Chang." She was asked to have a seat while they went to find him. A few minutes later, the person who greeted her returned with Mr. Chang.

Aiyana smiled, looked him in the eyes, and while speaking at a steady pace, extended her hand to him: "Good Morning, Mr. Chang, I am Aiyana, it is a pleasure to meet you and to talk about how Sunrise Property Services can help you with your marina improvements."

Mr. Chang seemed surprised to see her as his eyebrows went up and his walking towards her abruptly stopped. His shoulders tensed up towards his ears and his eyes wandered a bit looking around the room.

"Aiyana, nice - to - meet - you." he stated quietly as he slowly extended his hand for a shake. It was a firm professional handshake. "I was expecting Derek".

Aiyana didn't miss a beat and smiling confidently gave a brief introduction about herself and stated how she is focusing on the landscaping while Derek focuses on the trees.

She indicated that she was "sure he will see lots of Derek since he is still very much involved with all of his customers and that he really appreciates their business."

Mr. Chang relaxed his shoulders with her personable tone and her confident and calm demeanor. He recalled Derek mentioning that he had a new salesperson onboard at his last Lake Association networking event, but assumed it was Derek who would be on site today.

Aiyana and Mr. Chang made intermittent eye contact and smiled as they spoke. Mr. Chang noted she looked extremely friendly and relaxed. He also noted that she was dressed very formally and that she definitely wasn't from around here, comparing his casual golf shirt and khaki pants to her full business suit and high heels. No one does business like that around here, he thought.

Also, as a Chamber of Commerce member and strong supporter of local businesses, Eric just didn't feel like she represented "local" business. If he didn't know that she represented Derek's local company, he wouldn't have spoken with her about his landscaping needs.

They continued to speak for a few minutes, standing 2 meters apart. Then Aiyana asked if she could have a look at where in the marina he was considering the landscaping work. She expressed how beautiful his marina was and the gorgeous views he had with a big smile and big hand gestures.

Mr. Chang said "right this way" and extended his open hand out in the direction of the doors towards the lake. He opened the door and let Aiyana step out first. Aiyana took a few steps out and stumbled on the pea stone walkway. She instantly felt embarrassed as her heels sank into the soft gravel.

She tried to remain calm and professional as she stepped off the walkway and into the lawn where she tried to balance herself, although her heels sank into the grass as well. As she looked around, she noticed that everyone else was dressed very casually and that she was completely overdressed. She looked down and she could feel her cheeks flush with embarrassment.

Mr. Chang reached out a hand to help steady her, looked her in the eyes, and with a quiet voice tried to put her at ease by saying: "My wife, Suresha has a closet full of nice shoes she says that because of me, she has no place to wear anymore. We got married here at the marina 8 years ago, this is where we met. Suresha always tells me she knows she still loves me because she is still happy to sacrifice her nice shoes for practical ones."

Mr. Chang stopped speaking when he noticed that Aiyana was slouching and had turned away from him. He stepped back to give her space. She had crossed her arms and was staring blankly at the ground. Because she was recovering from her embarrassment, she has no idea what he just said, she hadn't heard him. She was silent and so was Mr. Chang.

Aiyana was mortified. She tried to stand up tall and regain her relaxed composure. She turned to face him, uncrossed her arms, repositioned her body towards him, made eye contact, raised her eyebrows, and with a wide smile, lifted her hands up to her shoulder with open palms facing him and said: "Thank you for helping me, I didn't expect to fall so hard for the lake view, it is beautiful" and they both have a little laugh.

"I apologize. I missed what you said during my recovery, can you please repeat it?" Mr. Chang happily shared his story again and Aiyana noted his wife's name for her notes later.

Aiyana re-directed the conversation back to the landscaping and she was able to ask a lot of questions and identify all of Mr. Chang's landscaping needs. It was a good, professional conversation and Mr. Chang was pleasantly surprised at how much she knew about landscaping. She had a few solutions in mind and they discussed a variety of possibilities. She noted the time and their scheduled meeting time was coming to an end in 5 minutes. She thanked Mr. Chang for considering Sunrise for the job and let him know that she would put some numbers together and have the office manager send over the quote as soon as possible.

She shook his hand firmly while smiling at him, said it was a pleasure to meet him and stated that she looked forward to meeting Suresha one day soon. She walked carefully to the car where she could reflect on her first in-person sales and site visit for Sunrise.

Also note that although there were a few rocky moments during Aiyana's sale visit, she managed to present a lot of positive non-verbal cues and had a positive impact on Mr. Chang and his sales experience. There were also some negative non-verbal cues that surfaced in the case. Let's review to address how some of those negative non-verbal cues can be turned into positive ones.

Aiyana was not Derek: Mr. Chang's non-verbal cues told Aiyana she needed to reassure him on her knowledge and skill, of the value he had as a customer and to also help him feel comfortable to begin building a relationship with Aiyana.

Aiyana was dressed too formally: Through appearance and clothing, she sent a formal message which was the expectation in Toronto, however, not in the Muskoka region where it is professional, but less formal.

Aiyana had an embarrassing moment when she stumbled: Aiyana began to shut down which she displayed through her body language by crossing her arms in front of her body, turning away and her poor posture. She was able to recognize this quickly and turned it around and continue to be a sales professional and strongly represent the company.

Bonus Content

If you have a further interest in this topic, watch the following video from actor and presentation expert, Julie Hansen and if you like, research similar topics online, like making eye contact or how to look comfortable on camera, to help you with your face-to-face and virtual selling approach.

Selling on Video, Julie Hansen (4:32):
https://www.youtube.com/channel/UC2fsQRv5pkcI7DIONE4yEEw

Networking Strategies to Connect with Other Businesses

Building rapport and relationships is an important part of building and maintaining a successful small business. It is essential to do so, not only with your current and potential customers but with the business community as well.

Business networking with other entrepreneurs is an essential component of a successful small business and can help you grow your customer base, generate referrals, and provide you with valuable learning, development and growth opportunities.

To build rapport and relationships within the business community, it is important to prepare yourself for making the most of every business networking opportunity. Being prepared will ensure that you make positive lasting impressions on not only your customers but on your peers within the business community as well.

Building and improving your networking strategies can help your small business, or the one you represent become a familiar name in the community and get you in front of current and potential clients.

Here are some examples of how to network within the community.

Practice Your Elevator Sales Pitch

When you get an opportunity to network, it is important that you are prepared when you get there to begin building relationships. An elevator pitch is a short influential speech to clearly explain your concept and generate interest. It is a great way to introduce yourself, your business, and how your products or services solve problems, for clients or other business owners.

Your introduction should be short, to spark interest. If you were in an elevator with someone for a few minutes, how would you capture their attention? This is where the name "elevator pitch" comes from.

In building relationships, you need to know your audience and although an elevator pitch is a great way to introduce yourself, you should have your base pitch created and then adapt it to every encounter when networking.

Reminder: Here are some suggestions on what could be in the framework of your sales pitch:

- Explain what your company does in laymen terms
- Explain how your company solve problems
- What makes your business unique
- Add some data to support your value
- Ask a question that engages the person you are speaking with. This could be a good conversation starter.
- Have your business card and contact information ready.
- Just keep trying, be patient. Although it is a form of a sales pitch, it is about building relationships in the business community.

Be an Active Chamber of Commerce Member – Attend their Events

The Chamber of Commerce is an organization that works locally to support businesses through networking and advocacy, and offers a variety of membership benefits. It is designed to help business owners in the same area connect with one another professionally. It offers small businesses access to a network of local business and specialized markets and provides valuable information on networking events and opportunities.

Every Chamber of Commerce has a directory of their members available to the community and is used by many potential clients and business in the area. Chamber of Commerce networking also offers a wealth of business experience and acumen from the members and staff with the potential of more clients or customers.

Industry or Community Associations You May Want to Join

Joining an industry or community association can offer local, regional and national range of opportunities to enhance and nurture relationships that can lead to great success.

Some of the industry associations offer membership leads and training, certification and licensing initiatives, access to industry events for networking, mentorship programs, vendor cost savings, and goodwill opportunities. There are community and national associations in all industries welcoming new members.

As an example of a community association, consider your local community sales networks or the Small Business Community Network (SBCN), an Ontario-based organization with many resources that could potentially add value to your small business enterprise: https://www.sbcncanada.org

Host a Client Event to Get Some Exposure

Consider hosting your own event. This is a great way for a small business to get exposure. This can be your business putting together an event that could attract potential clients and build rapport with others in the area. It could also be a collaboration between complementary businesses that could potentially partner in services or product and has similar networking goals.

An example of this would be if you are running a floral shop to co-host by connecting with a photographer, bakery and event rental business to showcase the business offerings while connecting with local business and potential clients. Some tips for hosting a successful networking event.

1. The People; you need not only a balance from the community but a respected guest speaker on an industry hot topic could draw people and focus the interest.
2. The Structure; A presentation or speaker creates focus, but the timing needs to be right. Keep 2/3 of the event for networking opportunities.

3. The Venue; It sets the tone for the event. Factors such as the right size, location, parking, ease of access all play a critical role in the success of the event.
4. Hospitality; Offering some food and beverages helps with attendance and eases guests
5. Host with the Most: Be hands on, greet everyone, introduce yourself and connect others through introduction.
6. Follow up; after the event, send out information to customers or business such as summary from your speaker. Keep looking for new business, partnerships and keep your current customers' attention flowing.

Have a Loyalty/Referral Program in Place

The best compliment to a small business is a referral. When you offer a positive experience for your customers and they trust you with their nurtured relationship, they will recommend you to their network. Having a rapport with your customers provides access to their networks informally. You could formally offer an incentive program such as a gift for successful referrals or a discount on future products or services encouraging your built relationships to help grow your network.

Networking and building business through relationships needs to be a balance in our digital world of social media and in person business networking. When you get an opportunity to network, it is important that you are prepared when you get there to begin building relationships for current or future sales.

Activity: Connecting with your Local Chamber of Commerce

This activity provides you with an opportunity to research and connect with your local Chamber of Commerce. Joining a chamber of commerce can help boost your sales and increase the visibility and credibility of your business.

This activity provides you with an opportunity to research and connect with your local Chamber of Commerce by follow the steps below:

Step 1: Research and determine what chambers are relevant to you and active in your area. Using your preferred search engine, type the name of your town/city, and the words Chamber of Commerce. Navigate the pages and confirm that these are your most relevant and local options.

Step 2: Once you have decided on a chamber or two that best fit your location and market, contact them to begin networking and determine your next steps.

Find the "contact us" section on their website and pick up the phone or send them an email to begin your networking.

Suggestions that you could include in your communication with the chamber.

- Introduce yourself
- A brief overview of your business
- Why you connecting with them (networking)
- Query about upcoming events to consider attending
- Any other questions that are relevant to your business or sales needs.

If you did join, then congratulations! This is a great step in building relationships and networking.

We challenge you to continue this process and encourage you to proceed with one or all of the items below.

- Attend an event
- Connect with a current member to gather insight on the chamber and how it can help you nurture relationships
- Join the chamber and set up your membership

Activity: Local, Regional, National Industry Associations

This activity provides you with an opportunity to research and connect with your industry. Joining an industry association can offer a local, regional and national range of opportunities to enhance and nurture relationships that can lead to great success.

This activity provides you with an opportunity to research and connect with one or more industry associations by follow the steps below:

Step 1: Research and determine what associations are available in your industry in your area, or at the regional or national level. Using your preferred search engine, type the name of your industry, the word: Associations and the name of your town, province or country. For example: Hotel Associations Regina OR Retail Associations Eastern Townships OR Sales Associations Canada. BE creative and find the most suitable ways to connect with industry professionals.

Step 2: Navigate to the "About Us" page and confirm that these are your most relevant options and that it would be a possible good fit for you or your company.

Step 3: Explore and navigate the pages for industry related topics, opportunities and conversations. It is a great place to explore and connect with like-minded professionals.

Step 4: Navigate to their events page. See if there are any events online or in-person that interest you and consider registering for them.

Step 5: Find the "Become a Member" or "Join Association" section on their website. If this is an association that you think will inspire you, assist your business and/or be a great networking opportunity, then register. You may have to complete a questionnaire or form. Determine if this is something that you want to do.

If you did join, then congratulations! You now have some new networking tools and connections to make. This is another great step towards building relationships and networking.

We challenge you to continue this process and encourage you to proceed with one or all of the items below to help build your network.

- Search for groups on LinkedIn for networking
- Look for industry publications and follow them online or subscribe for monthly publications.
- Search for networking groups by using some of your key industry words on Twitter

Bonus Content

If you have a further interest in topics around communication, consumer behavior, networking, and building rapport and relationships in sales, take the time to complete this BONUS content. It may help you gain some insight on the kind of consumer you are and help further your understanding of consumer behaviour and characteristics. It may even enhance your ability to interact with customers in your sales practices.

Visit the Strategic Business Insights website below and complete the US VALS survey.

Note that VALS (Values-Attitudes-Lifestyles) is a marketing tool used to predict consumer behavior based on their philosophical beliefs, mechanical and intellectual curiosity, among other things.

VALS segments adults into eight distinct types of consumers through psychological traits and key demographics that drive consumer behavior. The combination of motivations and resources determines how a person will express himself or herself in the marketplace as a consumer.

http://www.strategicbusinessinsights.com/vals/presurvey.shtml

Chapter Summary

In this chapter: Nurturing Relationships, you have learned about taking time to understand your clients and maintaining relationships over time that helps build brand loyalty and trust. If you nurture and build that relationship into a genuine connection, it can result in a mutually beneficial long-term relationship.

It is not about one sale, it's about all of the potential and future sales that customer, partner or business may be connected with. You are in the business of people regardless of your product or service, especially in B2C sales. Nurturing relationships matters.

Nurturing relationships can occur face-to-face, virtually, by telephone or through social media platforms. You have learned some techniques in communication styles, non-verbal communication, eye contact, developed strategies for networking and received a variety of industry tips for small businesses along the way. Relationships matter more than ever, and nurturing a customer-centric business relationship for long term sales goals can be mutually beneficial to any small business.

Chapter 3: Enhanced Communications in Sales

In this chapter you will be learning about active listening, how to respond to feedback and address complaints and use written communication to positively impact your sales strategies. You will also have an opportunity to build on techniques to help improve your listening skills and your responses to customers.

Enhanced communication is critical in today's sales environment. Taking time to understand your clients and to maintain relationships over time helps build brand loyalty and trust. If you nurture and build those relationships into genuine connections it can result in mutually beneficial long-term relationships which lead to more sales for your business. Sales success is not only about one sale, it's also about the potential and future sales that your customers, partners, and other businesses may be connected with. Regardless of your products or services, you are in the business of people, especially in a B2C sales environment. Through enhanced communication, you can send important messages about your business.

Communicating with clients to build relationships can occur face-to-face, or virtually, through video, telephone or as we build on in this module, social media platforms. In small business, relationships matter more than ever considering the continuing advancements in technology. Savvy buyers have more options available and having a brand voice in your communication through clear guidelines and policies, offers your customers with consistent messaging. You will find an easy-to-follow framework that will help you build timely responses to feedback.

The purpose of this module is to enhance your communication skills and adapt your selling strategies to help you respond confidently. Actively listening, responding to feedback, written customer-centric communication builds relationships for repeat business and referral.

Listening

Imagine yourself as the most knowledgeable salesperson within your organization. You have researched your product, the benefits and features of what you are selling and are confident in your competitive advantage. You have a great sales pitch, offer positive first impressions, and know how to use positive, open non-verbal and verbal behaviours. Based on all that, how effective do you think you could be in meeting your sales goals?

All the above are critical factors in sales communications and typically result in high positive outcomes. Now, take one more moment and imagine yourself as that highly-skilled salesperson with poor listening skills. Do you think that your sales would still be successful if you were not a good listener?

As it turns out, without this key communication component, your sales would most likely NOT be as successful.

Listening is a key component of the critical communication process we review in this course. Listening requires paying attention, and interpreting and remembering what was heard. Effective listening is a top requirement in a seller skill-set for success.

Activity: Listening Self-Assessment

Listening is an active process that requires continuous intention.

This short self-assessment of your listening skills is designed to help you prepare yourself for more positive sales interactions. Take some time to reflect on the questions and answer them as accurately as possible. After you have completed it, and as you work through the rest of this module, think about how the communication and relationship building concepts and ideas presented will help you in your practice.

To assess the effectiveness of your listening skills and to prepare for the best sales interactions you can have with prospects, customers or business contacts, complete the following self-assessment.

Read the Self-Assessment Statements in the left-hand column and select either Always, Sometimes or Never as your response.

To complete your self assessment, click the corresponding cell to indicate either Always, Sometimes, or Never. When you have completed the self-assessment, use the totals at the bottom of the table and add them together for your total score. Review your score against the Rating Feedback table. Depending on your responses and results, think about how you can improve your listening strategies as you work through the rest of this module.

Self-Assessment Statements	Always (5 points each)	Sometimes (3 points each)	Never (0 points each)
1. I listen carefully to what the customer is saying, even if I disagree with what they are saying			
2. When a prospect is speaking with me, I stop what I am doing and focus on what they are saying			
3. I avoid thinking about all of the work I need to complete when listening to others			
4. I ask for clarification when I am unsure of a customer's meaning			
5. When receiving constructive feedback on a product or service, I am open minded while listening			
6. To ensure I understood a client's meaning, I paraphrase			
7. Before forming a response to a customer, I wait until I have received the entire message			
8. I intentionally block out noises and other distractions while speaking with a customer			
9. I pay attention to non-verbal cues sent by the customer while I am listening			
10. I focus on general ideas, not the details when a client is speaking with me			
Totals			

Rating Feedback Table:

40-50 points: You have great listening strategies and these skills should continue to be applied to your sales interactions to help build relationships. But keep in mind, there is always room for improvement!

26-39 points: You have good listening strategies that will help you build sales relationships, but keep the areas for improvement in mind as you work through the module.

15-25 points: You have some listening skills for sales but they may not be enough for you to build and maintain solid customer and business relationships. The information in this module will provided you with some good opportunities to build your listening skills and strategies to help enhance your sales practice.

Below 15 points: You may be missing out on some great opportunities to build and maintain solid customer and business relationships by not focusing on the listening skills and strategies that can help you become a better salesperson. The information in this module may be of great value to your sales practice.

Good Listener / Bad Listener

Listening is an active process and requires continuous intention. It is more than just hearing what your customer is saying. Customers do not want to feel like a transaction. They want to be heard and they want to feel that their needs are being met through the connection that was built through the sale.

Listening is an area that has been identified as the largest weakness in sales representatives. (Acuff, 2006) Jerry Acuff and Wally Wood, The Relationship Edge in Business (Hoboken, NJ: John Wiley & Sons, Inc., 2006): 149–150;

Listening is important for salespeople because:

- Communication with customers cannot be effective without listening
- Good listeners learn more about their client than poor listeners
- Salespeople who are listening can help clarify meaning from the client
- Strong listening skills can stimulate more conversation with customers
- Salespeople who can listen for and quickly respond to hesitations, assumptions or information gaps have an advantage over those who cannot

Listening Process

Listening is an active, learned process and to be the best sales professional you can be, it is necessary to develop or improve your listening skills. The good news is that with practice and intention, everyone can develop or enhance their listening skills. In sales, it is the process of analyzing and decoding sounds into patterns and interpreting the meaning of the message by inferring understanding.

It is more than just hearing what your customer is saying, it is about being active in the process of listening.

- Hearing is the physiological process of receiving frequencies of sound through the ear canal.
- Listening involves four phases: Sensing, Interpreting, Evaluation, and Responding.

The SIER Model

Let's review the Steil, Barker, & Watson SIER model that presents the hierarchy of active listening and the steps required for effective active listening.

Listening is a hierarchical and sequential process. A person must have the lowest part of the pyramid before moving up the sequence of the listening process. When challenged with a listening breakdown, you need to go back to the lower levels in the hierarchy where the breakdown originated and take action to remedy to situation.

Source: Steil, L., Barker, L., & Watson, K. (n.d.). SIER Hierarchy of Active Listening. Provenmodels, accessed August 1, 2011, http://www.provenmodels.com/554)

The SIER Model

Sensing:

- This is the physiological process of hearing sound waves, seeing and receiving verbal and non-verbal messages and cues and sending them to the brain for interpretation or analysis. The analysis determines if action is required.
- If internal and/or external distractors are present, you may not receive your prospect's intended messages or cues.

Interpreting:

- After you've picked up the sounds and non-verbal cues, your brain focuses on and filters the information. During this process, information from those sounds and behaviours are sorted and decoded. This effort filters what is important for better focus on what you are hearing and seeing.
- In any situation, this is all very challenging with lots of sounds and cues coming in.
- It is particularly important in sales to remove as many distractors as possible such as closing doors, turning phones to silent and selecting quiet places to talk.

Evaluating:

- After you have decoded a message from the customer, the brain begins to assign meaning based on all of your past experiences and references. You will also sort fact from opinion, including logical and emotional components.

Responding:

- This relates to the feedback you provide to the client on how well the messages were received.
- The selection of responses and their appropriateness is critical in building relationships in sales. This includes the words you select, the delivery, and the timing, combined with all of the non-verbal signals.
- These factors all impact how your message is received and how you interpreted the information from your customer. Aligning your response with the best possible messaging delivery system, based on your customer's communication style should positively impact the sales interaction.

Active Listening

Active listening means listening completely. Whenever you get the opportunity to have a sales conversation, it provides you with the opportunity to have a prospect reveal information that will help you close the sale and build a long-term customer. It takes a lot of focus, energy and vulnerability to become great at listening, to become an active listener.

Four Qualities of Active Listening

1. Active listening involves non-verbal communication:
    a. Through your body language, you are showing that you are engaged in the conversation.
    b. You can pick up on your customer's messages, not only through the words they use but through their body language, gestures, facial expression and tone.
2. Active listening involves verbal communication:
    a. Make sure you ask your customers good questions, and really listen to their responses. Don't judge or make assumptions.
3. Active listening involves responding to what your client is saying:
    a. You can ask questions and follow up.
    b. Be sure to express emotions and speak confidently in your response.
4. Active listening includes keeping the focus on your customer – letting them speak:
    a. Prepare to have your prospect or customer be doing the talking as you listen
    b. To find interesting information about your clients, you need to be interested.

Mastering active listening skills requires you to be customer-focused and mindful of all verbal and non-verbal communication cues.

Understanding how you can best help your customer is the key to building positive relationships. And the only way to get to understand your customers and to know what they want is by listening to what they are saying. Good listening skills are also essential when you are receiving sales performance feedback or advice from those you respect in the industry.

Characteristics of a Good Listener

Remember, listening is an active process and requires continuous intention. Have a look at the following suggestions and samples on the characteristics of a good salesperson, as it relates to active listening and the overall process of listening.

The idea is to help ensure that your customers feel that their needs are being met through a connection and that they do not feel like a transaction.

Some of the samples may seem more obvious to you than others.

Good Listening Behaviours	Listening Skill (middle)	Bad Listening Behaviours
Interprets messages being delivered	Keep an open mind	Reacts to emotional words
Actively seeks common interests and opportunities for engagement	Seek out the customer's interests	Responds with information about you
Focuses on content and ideas that can assist clients	Focus on content, not delivery	Tunes out of conversations if subject matter is boring
Listens for a theme overview	Listen for ideas	Tunes in only to facts
Takes effective notes that capture bigger themes to present key ideas to customer	Be flexible	Takes too many notes, loses sight of client's bigger picture
Works hard at interpreting messages and listens between the lines	Work at really listening	Shows no focus and interest in client
Removes distractions to concentrate on customer	Avoid distractions	Is easily distracted with interruptions
Is inquisitive, curious and on a journey of learning new product information and benefits	Exercise your brain!	Avoids learning new things and new product information

How to Improve Listening Skills

If listening is an active, learned process then that means there is always an opportunity to become a better listener. Active listening is a key requirement to sales relationships because it helps to build trust through relational selling.

Practicing to improve your listening skills in sales, leads to higher sales performance. The reason? Through skilled, active listening you will be able to interpret a greater amount of your client's verbal and non-verbal cues.

As well as being able to pick up on, clarify and interpret the cues, you will also gain the critical ability to positively interact with your customers and enhance their experience by offering added benefits of positive influence based on their needs. When you demonstrate positive listening skills as a salesperson, it is directly associated with the customer's trust in you and the experience should result in continued sales and consumer loyalty.

Listening "Between the Lines"

We have learned in previous modules that the majority of messaging happens non-verbally through gestures, actions and behaviours of body movement. Listening "between the lines" is about taking these messages from your customer through their manners in conjunction with what is being said as you listen. Sales people who can use the information they are being told along with the information being sent through other means can typically develop a competitive edge. Observations and listening between the lines can prompt thoughtful responses to gain trust, understand needs and ask the right questions.

Taking time to be fully engaged in a conversation with your customers through the combination of actively listening and body language helps you send strong messaging and allows you to listen between the lines. In sales, having a competitive advantage is always a benefit.

Note that listening "between the lines" can also be associated with written communication. How and what people write can carry subtle messages and, as you will see later in this module, it is important that you read and respond with care and consideration.

Activity: Sunrise Property Services Meets Bob's Cottage Services Case Study

Read the following Sunrise Property Services Meets Bob's Cottage Services case study and identify the many POSITIVE characteristics related to active listening, good communication and, relationship building and networking present in the case.

You will observe some are related to ideas and concepts presented in previous modules of this course. Feel free to note those as well.

As you go through the following activity, think about how you would group the behaviours demonstrated into the following categories:

- Active listening strategies
- Good communication strategies
- Relationship building and networking strategies

When you have finished reading the Case Study, read the feedback below to reveal the areas of focus: POSITIVE characteristics of active listening, good communication and, relationship building and networking. See how they match to your own observations.

It was around noon when Derek grabbed a pizza to-go to share with his friend Eric Lee, a local marina owner. Derek wanted to ask Eric about how things went with Aiyanna and her first in-person sales meeting representing Derek's company, Sunrise Property Services. Derek was happy to get positive feedback about Aiyanna about her professionalism and knowledge. Eric also mentioned that there was a new arborist and landscaping company in town, Bob's Cottage Services. He met them yesterday after they dropped by the marina to introduce themselves. Derek had not yet met or seen Bob, but made a mental note to introduce himself and check out the competition.

On his way to his next job site, Derek noticed a truck parked on the side of the road with the "Bob's Cottage Services" logo and company name on it. Derek pulled over to introduce himself and chat with Bob to find out about him and his business, and his time in the Muskoka area. Bob seemed like a very open and friendly guy and the conversation went well. Derek was consciously making an effort to present himself positively through words and body language cues. He purposely left his phone in his truck to avoid distractions, and approached Bob with no judgements. Throughout the conversation, there was paraphrasing on both sides and Derek made a strong effort of "listening-between-the-lines" to what Bob was saying.

As it turned out, Bob and his sister Abby grew up in the area but moved away years ago. While Bob just recently moved back to Muskoka, Abby now owns Quick Dry Painting, a residential house painting company in Whitby. Because so many of Abby's customers in Whitby were cottagers in Muskoka, Bob and Abby were talking about partnering to offer house painting services in the Muskoka area. Bob said he liked working more on home improvements than as an arborist and landscaper because the demand seemed to be for larger jobs and he couldn't accommodate them due to his equipment limitations. As Derek drove away he thought about the new contact he made. Perhaps he was competition on smaller jobs but in the long run, there could be great potential for referrals for both of them . He was very happy he had stopped to say hello.

Feedback

It was around noon when Derek grabbed a pizza to-go to share with his friend Eric Lee, a local marina owner. Derek wanted to ask Eric about how things went with Aiyanna (Relationship building – follow-up on customer satisfaction) and her first in-person sales meeting representing Derek's company, Sunrise Property Services. Derek was happy to get positive feedback about Aiyanna about her professionalism and knowledge. Eric also mentioned that there was a new arborist and landscaping company in town, Bob's Cottage Services. He met them yesterday after they dropped by the marina to introduce themselves. (Communication, relationship building, networking) Derek had not yet met or seen Bob, but made a mental note to introduce himself (relationship building, networking) and check out the competition.

On his way to his next job site, Derek noticed a truck parked on the side of the road with the "Bob's Cottage Services" logo and company name on it. Derek pulled over to introduce himself (networking) and chat with Bob to find out about him and his business, (networking) and his time in the Muskoka area. Bob seemed like a very open and friendly guy (communication) and the conversation went well. Derek was consciously making an effort to present himself positively through words and body language cues. (communication – verbal and non-verbal) He purposely left his phone in his truck to avoid distractions, (active listening) and approached Bob with no judgements. (communication) Throughout the conversation, there was paraphrasing (active listening) on both sides and Derek made a strong effort of "listening-between-the-lines" (active listening) to what Bob was saying.

As it turned out, Bob and his sister Abby grew up in the area but moved away years ago. While Bob just recently moved back to Muskoka, Abby now owns Quick Dry Painting, a residential house painting company in Whitby. Because so many of Abby's customers in Whitby were cottagers in Muskoka, Bob and Abby were talking about partnering to offer house painting services in the Muskoka area. Bob said he liked working more on home improvements than as an arborist and landscaper because the demand seemed to be for larger jobs and he couldn't accommodate them due to his equipment limitations. (networking – potential referrals) As Derek drove away he thought about the new contact he made. (networking) Perhaps he was competition on smaller jobs but in the long run, there could be great potential for referrals for both of them (networking – potential referral). He was very happy he had stopped to say hello. (communication)

When Things Go Wrong

When a customer's expectations are met or exceeded on a product or service, the customer is satisfied with the outcome of the experience. But if promises on a product or service does not align with the reality of the customer's experience, there is a gap in the expectations of the sale.

Soliciting Feedback

Keeping the lines of communication open between all of your clients is critical for having opportunities to discuss any concerns and important issues. Encouraging feedback, both positive and negative can really benefit the business. There is lots of research on this, and it is generally believed that one quarter of your clients who have a problem will not complain. (McDargh, 2010 10.)

That is 25 percent of our business customers **NOT** letting us know that there was a problem. Scheduling periodic meetings after the sale gives the salesperson an opportunity to encourage feedback and ask candidly about the product or service being offered. Asking your clients direct questions opens the lines of communication that they may not have felt comfortable bringing forward themselves.

If you end up with negative feedback, you need to respond to resolve the issue to build trust and to continue to encourage feedback about your products or services. If your client's concerns are not responded to promptly and their expectations continue to be unmet, then trust is lost. You customer will likely not mention future concerns and if it continues, you could lose them to the competition. This is key to understanding authenticity in your sales strategy. If a complaint does occur during feedback solicitation, make sure you handle it in a professional, supportive way.

Dealing with Negative Feedback

It is every small business's desire to serve their customers and community successfully to encourage positive word-of-mouth feedback and referrals.

In sales, we want to know if there is a gap in the service or product experience compared to expectations. We want to encourage critical feedback. If we aren't making it easy for our customers to tell us of concerns, it could result in not being aware there was a problem and missing an opportunity to correct it for our customer or fix it for future customers.

Although we do not always consider hearing negative things from our customer as a good thing, consider the real value of this type of feedback. When you hear from a customer, if it is positive, it is an indication that you are doing a good job. But if the feedback is negative, then it is an opportunity for you to change what needs to be changed and head-off future complaints.

Being proactive and reducing negative experiences happens when small businesses have a system in place to track and monitor and communicate when a failure occurs. Analyzing this information helps make changes to reduce and eliminate customer gaps. When there is a gap in the experience for the customer, we need to make it right. What often results when you fix a problem and resolve the customer concern promptly, is the customer responds with additional business as you have proven your loyalty to them. Although customers complain about a variety of things, they tend to fall into these categories.

- Product performance
- Incorrect order
- Availability of product
- Late delivery
- Price variance
- Need more training on a product
- Unresponsive sales team
- Customers do not feel valued or validated

Remember that in sales, you are the face of the company and although not all of the above-mentioned items are the direct responsibility of the salesperson, the client is looking to you to fix the problem. You are their contact they have been building a relationship with and trust.

Buyers do not care who is to blame, they just want their problem resolved. Passing blame when a complaint arises can be detrimental to that long term relationship. The best response for the relationship is to address the complaint promptly, accepting responsibility and following up with the client while resolving the problem.

Positive Feedback

Although we are discussing negative feedback and its critical value to business and sales, there are also a lot of great things that come out of hearing positive feedback beyond just making us feel good. When we hear how our products or services are helping our customers, or how it exceeded expectations, it reinforces all the great things that come from a solid sales relationship and communication.

Positive customer feedback is an opportunity to celebrate, motivate and encourage everyone connected with your small business. It is an opportunity to identify your competitive advantage or to possibly stimulate innovation and growth. Knowing what is important to your customers can help you continue to build your small business.

The key to enhancing these relationships and growing your business, is to ask the right questions and solicit feedback (positive or negative) from customers and ensure that issues are addressed.

Bonus Content

Watch the following videos for some insight on power words and how you can choose the most suitable words and phrases when communicating with your current or potential customers.

VIDEO 1: Top Selling Words: How to Sell Better (The Psychology of Words in the Sales Process)

VIDEO 2: Tom Hopkins - Words That SELL

VIDEO 3: Speak Like a Leader – Simon Lancaster TEDxVerona

Resolving Problems

It is imperative that you do not overpromise and under deliver in sales. Being forthcoming and transparent about delivery dates, stock availability and all other areas of the product or service capabilities instead of just telling the client what they want to hear should avoid any disappointment.

Providing sales support can eliminate problems with late deliveries, incorrect orders, and unhappy customers. There are times when unexpected circumstances arise, outside of your control but communicating them quickly and professionally to the customer and providing options, helps keep them informed and able to prepare.

It is also critical to have some structure to your complaint handling to ensure all steps are completed. As the research suggests, if a company does not address a complaint brought forward and fails to address it with the customer and prospect, on average they will share their story with 10 people (Werner, 2013, 28-30).

Strategies for Handling Complaints

When you consider the different mass communication tools out there like television, email, social media and the general power of the Internet, not dealing with a customer complaint can result in an overwhelming amount of potential customers hearing negative things about your products or services.

So how can you use communication strategies to handle complaints? Have a look at the following suggested procedures and techniques for handling dissatisfied customers.

As you will see, the general strategy is to continue building those sales relationships for open communication, including complaints. These strategies include listening carefully, involving the customer in the resolution, keeping the customer informed and following up on solution satisfaction.

1. Addressing Complaints – Part of Open Communications

   Building sales relationships is about maintaining open communication for the sale, but is also means being open to dealing with complaints. The salesperson and customer, client or supplier must work together to continuously build trust to encourage comfort levels in speaking up. Having open communication channels will encourage conversation. This does not always need to be formal, but should be formalized for consistency.

2. Conducting regularly scheduled sales calls, follow up calls and visits after the sale at different intervals allow the client to experience the different things with the product. An example of this may be a customer satisfaction call 1 week, 30 days and 60 days post sale. Sales team members must be comfortable asking questions such as:
   - How was your experience?
   - How did we do?
   - Do you like the product?

- Was it everything that you expected?
- Would you buy it again?
- Anything that I can help with or you wanted to discuss?

When you regularly connect with customers, you are sending them a message of care and concern. You are serving their needs well and this is critical in building loyalty in small business.

3. Listening Carefully for the Entire Story

As discussed earlier in the module, listening to our customers is a key component of communication.

Use the skills addressed to extract as many details as possible and get a full understanding of their story and experience. This helps you serve them best for a resolution. Make the customer feel comfortable bringing things forward. Thank them for giving you an opportunity to hear their concerns. Let them tell their story, without interruptions. Recall from previous learning that listening involves four phases:

- sensing, interpreting, evaluation, and responding.
- Listening between the lines for the entire story with the combination of the spoken and unspoken messages being portrayed so you who can use the information through observations to understand their needs and offer the best solution.
- Once the customer has expressed their complaint, respond with appropriate feedback and questions.
- The selection of responses and its appropriateness is critical in building relationships in sales and resolving the concerns. Remember, this includes the selection, delivery, and timing of your words combined with your non-verbal cues. Make sure they are aligned showing empathy and a solution-based approach.

4. Including the Customer in the Resolution

Instead of attempting to guess what the customer feels is an appropriate resolution, it is beneficial to ask and understand what their needs are. As you may recall, there is a variety of customer styles and behaviours, as well as a variety of needs and wants. The range of solutions can include being heard, apologies, discounts, or alternatives.

Once a salesperson is aware of what their customer wants, they then must agree on a solution.

Remember, it should be a customer-focused solution, not a salesperson solution. If what the customer has asked for is an available option, it should be met. If it is not possible, you can offer similar solutions and the options available. Once you know what they would like, offering 2 options is a way to put the customer in control of selecting their best solution. Choice allows the customer to have an increase in perceived control, ultimately leading to higher satisfaction. (Chia-Chi Chang, 2006, 203).

5. Keeping the Customer Informed

Take action on the agreed solution to resolve promptly. Keep the customer informed and be as transparent as possible as knowledge is power for your clients. They can make the decisions they need to base on the information they are provided. Communicate timing, the steps that have been acted upon and what to expect next. Keep them informed along the solution journey until completed.

6. Following-Up on Solution Satisfaction

After the solution is identified and the problem is resolved, the salesperson typically schedules a follow up call to ensure that the customer is satisfied with the solution. This is an opportunity to not only confirm that the customer is happy with the solution, it also demonstrates that you truly care about their business. Following up also gives you another opportunity to possibly solicit referrals.

Written Communication

The words you chose during your verbal communications with customers and business contacts have a powerful impact on your sales outcomes – so does your written communications.

Like verbal communication, written words hold a lot of power and will impact how you make people feel. The verbal and written words you use in selling not only communicate information about your products or services, they also communicate powerful messages about you as salesperson and the company you represent.

When using written communication for sales and business purposes, it is in your power to be positive in that communication. And if you want to make sales, you need to choose the most suitable words and maintain a positive language. The goal is to choose the words that build positive relationships through trust building and motivating the customer to say yes to a sale.

Many of the techniques you learned in verbal communication, apply to written communication. Let's look at some strategies related to written communications in sales.

Professional Sales Writing

Writing professionally with appropriate language, grammar and sequencing are all parts of communicating in writing. When proposals, emails, presentations and social posts are riddled with poor grammar, the credibility of the message is lost. The leader will focus on the errors instead of the content and it will not be considered as very professional.

It is equally important to have the message flow in a way that the reader can understand all parts of the written message. The intention of written communication is to send information and should be presented in a logical order for the reader for better understanding. If the message is jumbled and hard to navigate, the person you are communicating with will not understand your message. The facts and details need to be organized and presented to the reader in clearly written communication. Prior to writing, prepare an outline of all key points of communication and their flow and always check your grammar and spelling.

Using the general terms and vocabulary that is most appropriate for your target market will help to ensure the clarity of your message.

Email Signatures and Automatic Replies

We discussed the importance of writing professionally with appropriate language, grammar and sequencing and this includes signatures. Often, a majority of written sales communication occurs through emails and it is important when composing an email that it has a signature. Each email provider will have a function in settings that allows you to create a signature that will automatically attach at the end of your email.

An email signature should include at a minimum; name, position, company, company logo, contact information. This creates credibility and provides critical information for the customer.

Another professional requirement for emails is to use the automatic reply functionality within your email settings when you are away from the office. Your automatic reply should contain; out of office heading, greeting to the customer, dates of your absence, you expected return date, and who to contact as an alternative in your absence. This automatic reply provides a communication to the customers about when they can anticipate a response to their query and provides them with an alternative to ensure they have options if a resolution is required that cannot wait until your return.

Written Sales Proposals

A written sales proposal is a targeted self-contained sales presentation. It is often partnered with additional sales dialogue, well organized, customized information targeting a potential client based on how your business can assist them. It is often used in quotes and bidding scenarios for a selection process. Sales proposals are typically written formally for the clients review in their decision making process. Proposals should be written clearly, be informative and include details such as value proposition, pricing, technical information, schedules or timelines and a commitment request for proposed contract.

Creating Consistency in Written Communication

More and more customers are using social media to connect, communicate and research small businesses. Potential and current customers use many devices daily including computers, phones, tablets for mobile, social and digital communication.

Business is also selling socially digitally by leveraging of all of these devices to communicate, get feedback, provide information, network and engage current and potential customers. Representing the company aligned with goals, ethics and brand direction should always be a priority. Once communication is sent to digital platforms, how the communication is viewed and shared is out of your direct control.

Having a communication policy in place at your business can provide clearer guidelines in all areas of written communication and can offer a consistent voice for your company's written communications like email, social media, social selling and proposals. Such policies can help guide everyone within the organization in areas such as required response times, templates, tone of the responses, and who should be responding to what.

Online Communication

Just as customers are using social media to connect, communicate and follow their favourite products and services, potential customers also research and read reviews and other digital communication to make purchasing decisions. The stronger a company's social presence online, the greater the need to monitor and respond and customers. Having strong social media response guidelines will help with consistent responses and send the right messaging to your customers and potential customers.

Building relationships can happen through a strong, consistent digital presence. Responding to customer reviews make the customer feel appreciated, can promote further engagement and even strengthen your relationship with them. Potential customers who can see responses to reviews can make more informed purchasing decisions based on their perception of how important your customers are to you in those responses. How you make people feel online through your written communication can determine future sales.

Responding to positive reviews helps you thank your customers and promote your business. Responding to negative reviews can help manage your online reputation, fix problems and provide enhanced information.

How to Respond to Online Reviews

There are many positives to writing a response to a customer review. It is very natural to get excited about a customer's positive experience with your business, just as it is natural to feel upset when a customer writes a negative review. Responding to negative reviews with calm professionalism is always an important part of building positive relationships. The words you use in your responses not only communicate information about your products or services, they also communicate powerful messages about you as a salesperson and the company you represent.

As part of your communication policy, a response framework can provide guidance and professionalism in your responses to online feedback and comments. Let's review some of the main parts of a response framework for both negative and positive reviews.

Responding to Positive Reviews	Responding to Negative Reviews
Personalize the response	Personalize the response
Thank the customer for their business	Thank the customer for feedback
	Apologize
Respond in a timely manner	Respond within 24 hours
Be specific	Keep the response short and professional
Encourage using your business again	Avoid defending your business
	Invite offline communication, if necessary
	Include contact information

Framework for Responding to Customer Feedback

Let's take some time and work through a framework for responding to a negative review. Please note, with the exception of moving the discussion offline, this framework can be used for in-person feedback and responses as well. You will have an opportunity to practice this, so take notes and work through each step of the framework.

Personalize the response	Address the reviewer by name, but if you cannot find their name, choose their online reviewer name. This is a great relationship building technique for responding to a c... digitally or in person, and helps personalizes your response.	
Sample response	(If it was user ABC123 who wrote the review) "Dear ABC123,"	
Appreciate the feedback	Thanking the customer sets a positive friendly tone that they and other potential customers will read.	
Sample response	"Thank you for taking the time to write the review and telling us about your experience."	
Acknowledge the feedback	This is an important step in the communication as it confirms the reason the review was written. You can do so by paraphrasing and validating the customer's experience.	
Sample response	"We are sorry you did not have a quality experience with our product."	
Apologize with accountability	Show the customer that you care about them and their experiences. Offering an apology shows you are accountable to your business and customers. Keep this brief and p...	
Sample response	"We hold ourselves and our products to high expectations, I am sorry that was not your experience."	
Offer a solution	Each customer has a unique experience. The solutions you offer them should also be customized to their experiences. Briefly bring up the customer's concerns and highlig... will improve the situation or the experience for the customer. Continue to be accountable and resolve the issue.	

If we pull all the framework pieces together, this could be the full response:

Dear ABC123,

Thank you for taking the time to write the review and telling us about your experience. We are sorry you did not have a quality experience with our product. We hold ourselves and our products to high expectations, I am sorry that was not your experience. We pride ourselves on our customer's satisfaction, we want to make it right and ensure you have a great product experience. We can replace the product and have it sent to you immediately, or we could offer you an exchange or refund, I am here to make it right. I would like to ensure a quick resolution and an opportunity to further understand your feedback. Please contact me at guest-servicesmanager@company-name.com or call me at 555-123-4567 to ensure your satisfaction as quickly as possible. Thank you again for your feedback and giving us the opportunity to make it right. We appreciate your business.

Sincerely,
your Name,
Name of your business

Through practice you will become very comfortable responding to reviews and responding to your customers that have had a positive and negative experience. Businesses that have clear guidelines help remove some of the stress of responding in a timely manner.

Let's take some time and review the benefits of using templates to respond. When training team members on expectations of responses, it is recommended that you have framework that represents your business needs as a reference and guideline.

Templates for Responding

Templates will help guide you in responding. Although they can be helpful, you also want to avoid writing the same response to all for your reviews. It is suggested that you have multiple templates and that you rotate them. I think you will find after several responses; you will naturally follow the guidelines without referring to your templates any longer.

There are some great resources that break down the types of reviewers and even offers some suggested templates for responding to each of the customer types. A template can help guide your responses and maintain professionalism. Here are two examples, in a blog by Andew McDermott, and another by Chatmeter.

Not only will you find some templates here, you will also see some great reasons as to why they can be effective when used at the right time.

https://blog.grade.us/review-response-templates-negative-reviews/

https://www.chatmeter.com/blog/10-review-response-templates-you-can-use-right-now/

Bonus Content

Here are some great websites with additional review response information to help you and your business establish a response policy:

https://www.godaddy.com/garage/the-best-tips-for-responding-to-online-reviews/

https://www.businessnewsdaily.com/9187-respond-to-online-reviews.html

https://www.reviewtrackers.com/guides/examples-responding-reviews/

https://www.vendasta.com/blog/how-to-respond-reviews-good-bad/

https://hbr.org/2020/05/5-principles-for-responding-to-customer-reviews

https://help.gatherup.com/s/article/Responding-to-client-objections-about-online-reviews

Chapter Summary

In this chapter, you have learned about active listening and techniques to improve your listening and response skills. If you can learn to listen effectively, listen "between the lines", ask the right questions and respond appropriately to your customers, it should result in a mutually beneficial long-term relationship. Especially in B2C sales, you are in the business of people regardless of your products or services. Enhancing your sales communication skills will make a difference.

The enhanced communication techniques related to listening, responding and written communications you have learned here can be used face-to-face, virtually, by telephone or through social media. These enhanced communications will help ensure that you send messages as intended, that you respond appropriately to positive and negative feedback and that you know what to do when things go wrong.

Chapter 4: Meetings and Presentations

Introduction

In this module you will be learning about meetings and presentations. In sales, you will have several opportunities to provide information to your customers about how your products or services could benefit them. You want to motivate them in an effective way through strong communication in your meetings and presentations to convert the sale. All the communication skills you learned throughout this course can be brought together to help you build strong business relationships through your sales meetings and presentations.

Matching appropriate meeting and presentation formats and platforms with the identified needs of your customers and business contacts is a large part of the skills required for sales success. Identifying the tools and techniques used to present your products or services during a meeting is also part of that success.

In this module, you will learn to build the skills needed for preparing meetings and presentation agendas, working with templates that can help you set up organized and professional meetings.

Building relationships is critical in today's sales environment. Taking time to understand your clients and to maintain relationships over time helps build brand loyalty and trust. Building those relationships into genuine connections can result in mutually beneficial long-term relationships which lead to more sales for your business. Managing and maintaining information collected from your meetings and planning post-meeting follow ups will also help grow those relationships.

Sales success is not only about selling part of a meeting or presentation, it's also about the potential for future sales and referrals. Regardless of your products or services, you are in the business of people, especially in a B2C sales environment. Maintaining contact through follow ups and skillful connection points demonstrates a solid customer-focused sales approach.

The purpose of this module is to enhance your meeting and presentation preparation skills and confidence and to adapt your selling strategies in ways that will help you nurture your business relationships, potentially leading to an increase in your sales. Remember, building trusting, customer-centric relationships for repeat business and referrals is the optimal goal.

Meetings

Whether your small business is having a meeting with clients or business contacts, or you are meeting internally, establishing some best practices in those meetings can help enhance the outcomes.

Meetings play a key part in communication in sales. They are an opportunity to build your skills, reputation and business relationships. There will be times when you will need to collaborate with your team, host a sales call, interact with prospects or repeat customers and when these happen, being prepared will always increase your chances for success.

Meetings take all forms and purposes, and according to MeetingSift, they fall into 6 main categories:

1. Status Updates
2. Information Sharing
3. Decision Making
4. Problem Solving
5. Innovation
6. Team Building

Information Sharing

For the purpose of this module and with a focus on sales, we will be focusing on the meeting category of Information Sharing.

After all of your hard work during the prospecting phase of the sales cycle, your goal is to nurture your sales or business relationships. Meetings and presentations are your opportunities for building and nurturing these relationships.

Note that some of these techniques and challenges were covered the Prospecting and Pipeline Management course and will be covered in more detail here.

All business requirements are different and what motivates your customers will be just as unique as what motivates you and your business goals. You are encouraged to take the guidelines in this module and personalize them for your small business needs and experiences.

Sales meetings typically happen in two formats: in person or virtually. The guidelines in this module will apply to both these formats. But regardless of the format, the type of meeting required will dictate the details around it, such as the objectives, environment, agenda, formalities, timing, etc. Let's start with meeting objectives.

Successful Meeting Tips

These tips will help you plan, prepare and conduct great meetings to share valuable information and to help you get your message across. They are linked to the meeting agenda, covered later in this module. Think about the connections as you go through the content.

(1) Accessibility

If your meeting is online, provide the meeting link at the time of scheduling and as a reminder the dayprior to your scheduled meeting. Including this directly along with any required instructions in theinvitation makes it easy for the customer to join the call. It demonstrates that you are organized and itreduces any stress of accessing the call for the customer, such as looking through emails and wonderinghow to connect.

(2) Timing

Start the meeting on time. Everyone is busy and has full schedules. Respect the client's time at the startof the meeting and by ending the meeting at the scheduled time. This demonstrates that you value and respect their time.

(3) Engagement

Encourage conversation and interaction with the customer by asking questions with the intention of identifying their needs and challenges. This interaction builds rapport but also helps you understand your customer and helps tailor your communication with them. This interaction also helps you identify their buying motives. This refers to the most important factors from the customer's perspective in making a purchasing decision. The best type of questions to ask when information sharing are open ended which encourages the customer to speak and share.

(4) Review

Prior to ending a meeting, review the main findings and objectives moving forward and the next steps. This helps clarify that you and the customer have the same understanding of the meeting outcomes.

This also helps gain some form of commitment. As you recall from the video, George clearly missed this opportunity in his meeting.

(5) Follow Up

As part of the follow up process, circle back with the customer as soon as possible to thank them and keep yourself top of mind. Note that this will be discussed in more detail later in the module.

The Environment

Where the meeting is held can contribute to the overall impression of your business and the products or services you sell. When hosting a sales meeting, it is important that the environment is taken into consideration. If you have a meeting space, you want it to build a positive impression. If you do not have a designated meeting area, your office or wherever you plan to meet should be tidy and presentable.

Typically, a preferred type of meeting areas is open, clean and bright since this can give the impression of being more welcoming than a dimmed unkempt area. Have a look at the images below. Where would you prefer to meet?

Would your first impression be the same for these two meeting locations? Do you think that it would impact how confident you were in the meeting?

Now put yourself in your customer's shoes. Where do you think a client would be most comfortable attending a meeting? If the space is clean and bright, does it give the client the same feeling as the meeting space that is dark and messy?

In small business, space can be limited and there may not be a dedicated meeting room resulting in meetings being hosted in your office or the common area of your facility. The same principles apply. Try to keep your space organized and clutter free to provide an impression of professionalism and organization at all times.

Virtual Meeting Background

Virtual sales calls and meetings occur frequently and are a more convenient way to maintain relationships and stay connected with your clients. The ambiance and environment during virtual meeting should be taken into consideration.

Often times these can be done from home or in the office space. Wherever you have the meeting, the background, as well as other possible distractions should be taken into consideration. This includes background noise such as electronics, pets and children.

If, for example you are in a common space, you could select a blurred background or place a personalized company background electronically into your meeting platform, eliminating the client's view of the actual space. If you are in a home office or workplace office, you could do the same or position yourself in a location where the camera can view a neat and tidy space offering a more professional impression. Make sure the space is bright and you are easily visible during your call (not just the top of your head).

Formalities

When it comes to formalities around meetings, there is not a one size fits all formula or rules around this in terms of dress code and behaviours. It is dependent on many factors, including your customers. As you grow to know your customers and with the information you collect on them, you will know how to deal with formality issues in terms of dress code and behaviour.

One thing that should always be formalized is your preparedness and preparation prior to your meetings. As a salesperson, your intentions are to communicate as effectively as possible about the meeting objectives, to share information and to build relationships. Finding that balance of formality will help you set the tone and pace of your meetings.

Sales Call Agenda

A successful sales call doesn't just happen. You typically cannot just wing it. In order to present yourself as organized and focused, you need to plan and prepare. An agenda helps you do this. When you take time to formalize your agenda, it helps you organize your sales activities, and displays professionalism. Agendas should be used for both in-person and virtual meetings.

Whether an agenda is shared with the person you are meeting or not, it should be prepared and followed so that you can manage the time, meet objectives, and share key information. It also helps you review the information you gather and make sure you didn't miss anything. An agenda demonstrates the professionalism of the sales representative and the company.

Once you develop an agenda format that works for your sales strategy and calls, it can be adapted for all your contacts. Itis a great tool to use for taking notes that you can add to your customer profiles for follow ups and continuous relationship building.

There are three major components of a sales agenda: You planning strategy, your meeting agenda flow, and your post meeting checklist items.

Pre-Meeting Plan

Research your contacts and try to identify how your products or services could help them. Remember that you are establishing rapport and building a relationship. You want to determine how you can help them with your product or service.

Confirm the meeting time with the person you're meeting in order to schedule the meeting location or virtual platform and then provide all connection details through a meeting request that includes the meeting location, or if the meeting is virtual, the online connectivity information. This confirmation could also include important details such as parking, access to the building and any other information to ensure your contact's ease and comfort. You want the customer to feel they have all of the required information to meet with you. Your goal here is to build trust early by showing how organized and prepared you are. Eliminating any questions preemptively does this.

As you create an agenda for the meeting, you will want to identify your meeting objective, expected pace and timing, topics to cover and questions for the customer. Allow space in the agenda to take notes, recap, to determine next steps and action items, and record all other meeting details.

Meeting Flow Plan

During the meeting you will want to be sure to have some formalities in place to keep the meeting flowing and professional. Think about what you've learned in this and the other modules in this course, like interpersonal communication, verbal and non-verbal communication and listening skills. You will be expected to use these skills throughout your meetings.

Some suggestions for a natural flow of the meeting would be to welcome attendees and thank them for their time. You will introduce yourself and any associates joining the meeting. Allow the customer to introduce themselves.

Communicate your meeting objective and try to seek out facts and information through open ended questions to help build rapport with the customer and encourage their participation. This fact finding technique can help you identify how you can help them meet their goals or solve problems.

During the meeting you will communicate your customer value proposition (sales pitch), and if relevant, offer the customer supporting materials and information packages about your products or services and identifying how you can meet their needs.

In these planning stages, you should be prepared to answer all possible questions and respond to objections. Take some time to anticipate these and prepare responses, this can help increase sales meeting success.

After communicating how you can help the customer, take the time to listen to their questions and "read between the lines" of what they are asking. Answer their questions and also ask for feedback or input. This is an important step as it builds rapport and allows you to extract information through active listening to better understand their needs, timing requirements and their motivation to make a decision.

Once you've covered your discussion items, summarize and review the action steps needed along with the next steps, schedule a follow up meeting, and thank the customer for their time.

Below you will find the suggested items in an easily accessible meeting agenda and presentation template for your use.

Post-Meeting Plan

After the meeting, it is important to record the meeting details and information extracted from the customer, and place information in your customer profile and customer relationship management database for ease of access and follow up in the future. Expanding on your notes and including them as part of your records will help you recall specifics about the customer and their unique needs. This is a great time to schedule any action items that were identified. Within 24 hours, follow up in writing with a thank you and acknowledgements from meeting such as any data, clarifications or addressing any concerns that were raised. Respond to all follow up requests promptly and professionally.

Using a Sales Call Agenda and Checklist

A sales call agenda template can be aligned with your customer relationship management (CRM) data input or integrated into your software system, if you are using CRM software.

This simple and accessible meeting agenda and checklist template summarizes all the key points just discussed to help you plan, organize and prepare your upcoming meeting agendas. Click the link above to download the template.

Sales Call Agenda and Checklist Template

Contact Information

- ☐ Customer Name:

- ☐ Date of the Meeting:
- ☐ Meeting location/connection link:
- ☐ Attendees:

Pre-Meeting Plan

- ☐ Research your contact and try to identify how your product/service could help them (problem solver)
- ☐ Write questions you'd like to address
- ☐ Define topics to discuss
- ☐ Estimate timing to help stay on schedule per topic (include time for Q&A)
- ☐ Create Agenda
- ☐ Schedule meeting location or virtual platform
- ☐ Send meeting request through calendar function, if possible (include online connection information)
- ☐ Confirm meeting time
- ☐ Communicate meeting details such as location, room name, parking options, etc.
- ☐ Send Agenda to key attendees, as required

Meeting Flow Plan

- ☐ Welcome attendees and thank them
- ☐ Introduce yourself and other business representatives joining you (note how you want to do this)
- ☐ Allow customers to introduces themselves
- ☐ Communicate reason for meeting (note your reason for the meeting)
- ☐ Introduce your topics and time frame for each
- ☐ Initiate Fact-Find and Rapport questions to identify how you can help them meet their goals (list your main questions)
- ☐ Extract information through open-ended questions to understand their needs, timing, and motivation
- ☐ Communicate your customer value proposition

- ☐ Provide supporting materials and information about product/service, as required
- ☐ Align how your product/service can help them meet their needs (identified earlier)
- ☐ Answer questions from customer
- ☐ Ask for feedback or input from the customer
- ☐ Review follow up actions needed and next steps and summarize
- ☐ Schedule next meeting/steps

Post Meeting Plan

- ☐ Record meeting details and keep records for future meetings and customer relationship management
- ☐ Schedule any action items in your calendar to meet the deadlines
- ☐ Within 24 hours, follow up in writing with a thank you and summary from meeting (information, requests)
- ☐ Respond to all follow up requests promptly and professionally.

Notes Area:

Activity: Preparing for a Sales Call: Template Search & Development

This activity will help you research and develop a template that you can use to prepare for your sales calls.

Take some time to investigate how you can best prepare for a sales call by researching and finding templates that can help you, as a salesperson, plan and prepare for your sales calls.

There are a variety of tools available to you that you can customize for your small business sales needs that will help you build your customer relationships.

Some suggested online search topics are:

- Sales planning templates
- Sales call agenda templates
- Planning a sales call and presentation, etc.

Based on the template provided, Sales Call Agenda and Checklist Template, and the ones you found through your online search, put a template together that would help you conduct successful meetings with potential customers. If you already use one in your sales activities, see how you can improve your current one with what you have learned.

Your Agenda template should, at a minimum, have 3 sections:

- Pre-Meeting Plan
- Meeting Flow Plan
- Post-Meeting Plan

Determine what to add within the sections of your template and how you will address your particular requirements.

Activity Feedback

These searches will generate a variety of responses where you can see some best practices that will help you customize a template that works best for B2C sales model needed for your sales calls.

Remember, your Agenda template should, at a minimum, have 3 sections: (1) Pre-Meeting Plan (2) Meeting Flow Plan (3) Post-Meeting Plan.

In addition to what your online search provides, review the content in this module to ensure you have addressed all requirements.

Suggested Prep Work:

Test and refine your template by preparing for a meeting with someone who could provide you with feedback or a think of a fictitious customer to help you work through any problem areas before completing this activity.

Meeting Platforms

In-person face to face meetings make it the easiest to build relationships. The next best thing is a virtual face-to-face meeting. Sales calls and meetings can be very effective in helping you become connected, stay connected and exchange information in an efficient and timely manner. With the popularity of communicating virtually, there has been a rise in the amount of meeting platforms available. Most of the virtual platforms allow for audio, video, document sharing and the access on a variety of devices makes most of them affordable for small business.

There is no doubt that there are a lot of options out there and you need to consider what is best for your business. A simple search can yield hundreds of options. Below you will find a link to some sites that offer a summary on some of the "top" meeting platforms including a summary on their features and benefits.

Below, you'll find a rundown by Ty Collins, on Calendly on the best video conferencing software they suggest grouped by category. Hopefully, this will help you make an informed choice: https://calendly.com/blog/online-meeting-platforms/

You can also have a look at suggestions by Kierra Benson with Tech Funnel, including a summary of their offerings and direct links to their sites: https://www.techfunnel.com/information-technology/11-best-virtual-meeting-platforms-for-business/

Features to Consider in Meeting Platforms

There are a variety of features you should consider when identifying which meeting platform will work best for you. According to Kierra Benson at Tech Funnel, when considering such software purchases, you should consider the following for your small business needs:

Insight: Does it meet your current and potential future needs? Ensure the virtual meeting platform that you choose to use has features the can accommodate.

Dependable: Consistency in quality and high-resolution visuals allows for smooth meetings that can increase your productivity and add value for the customer.

Desktop Sharing: An important aspect of a sales meeting is not just being able to see each other, but having the ability to interact and showcase information in real time.

Video Conferencing: This is the main feature that a virtual meeting platform must have in order for online sales meetings to take place.

Communication Options: Tools for communication and sending additional links and information such as chat and instant messaging allows easy transfer of information and can be synced with other technology.

Links and Easy Sign-On button: Is it easy for a customer to log on and connect? Keep it simple and easy and stress free.

Source: https://www.techfunnel.com/information-technology/11-best-virtual-meeting-platforms-for-business/

Follow Up After a Meeting

As a sales person, follow up should be one of your top priorities for effectively building relationships and confirming sales. The main intention of the follow up is building relationships, interacting, connecting and demonstrating your knowledge about how you can help them with your product or service in an honest and open way. Customers buy when they are ready and you want to be communicating after a sales call to find a time that works for them to close the sale.

Follow Up After a Meeting

Follow up as soon as possible after the meeting to keep you and your product or service top of mind.

Within the follow up, you should include:

- Thank you: thank them for meeting and their time.
- The main takeaways from the meeting, including a summary of the key areas discussed and how your product/service could help them.

- Your action items - what your next steps are going to be.
- Their next steps.

Following Up (Building Relationships)

As mentioned earlier, your sales follow up should have the intention of building relationships, interacting, connecting and demonstrating your knowledge about how you can help them with your product or service in an honest and open way.

Let's have a look at how your follow ups can enhance those customer relationships:

Interacting: Optimize the contact points with the customer to encourage conversation and engagement between yourself and the customer

Connecting: In sales you should connect and build relationships to influence purchasing decisions based on how you can help solve problems. Ensure you are consistent with your commitments and communication to build trust and dependability.

Demonstrating Knowledge: It is your job as a salesperson to qualify through questions and feedback on how you and your products can best help your customer. Your role is to develop insights into how you can customize each customer situation and requirements. Find out how to best help the customer through gaining knowledge of their needs.

Being Relatable: Use the techniques in the previous modules with interpersonal and enhanced communication skills on creating value to the customer interactions and developing relationships to maintain relevance and value.

Presentations

When you think of a sales presentation, you may consider it a simple pitch with facts and figures, or a demonstration of your product. Although these are components, the presentation is a combination of these items visually to support your objective of communicating information on how you can add value to the customer with your product or service.

Done effectively, with planning and the right timing in your sales process, it will capture your prospect's attention, creating value and motivation to make a buying decision.

It is important to acknowledge here, that everything reviewed in the first part of the module with regard to meetings is applicable to presentations. This part of the module will highlight some key considerations for presentations.

Components of a Presentation

Organized sales communication, dialogue and presentations can be adapted to enhance the effectiveness of interactions with customers. When you can learn about your contact's needs and customize solution-based messages, it can motivate the customer. Personalizing the sales presentation and minimizing a canned or contrived approach demonstrates effort and builds towards trust.

When planning a presentation, using a planning template is a good idea. The template provided earlier in the module and the additional examples you curated in your activity search are tools to ensure you prepare and organize the best communication for your contacts. These tools help you present a solution to the customer and learn as much as possible about. Presentations are a great way to motivate the customer through showcasing your customer value proposition.

Focusing on Your Message During a Presentation

When preparing a sales presentation, the focus is on communicating information to your customers or network to build relationships. The message needs to be what they need to hear. A focused customer message will keep you communicating professionally to meet their needs. Below are some key points that will help you concentrate on a customer focused message.

    a. Maintain positive verbal messages that are relationship building and indicate you are there for the customer.
    b. Offer open body language to communication and avoid non-verbal barriers such as crossed arms or placing items in between you and the customer.

c. Offer confident posture; sit straight and square your shoulders to your customer. Look alert and lean forward slightly.
d. Offer opportunities for discussion and engagement on the information and topics.
e. While in person, position yourself to have visual lines with all people present / For virtual meetings make sure you look into the camera at all those present as often as you can
f. Prepare questions for interaction to get to know your network contacts and customers
g. Demonstrate high energy and involvement.
h. Follow your agenda items including topics, your start/end times, order of the items, and opportunities for questions and conversation.

Customer Value Proposition

During your presentations, you want to capture the customer's attention with a good customer value proposition. The Customer Value Proposition is your explanation of why and how a customer benefits from choosing your products or services. It should be a direct and simple statement that you customize and include in your presentation.

Focus on the benefits that motivate your customer. Your Customer Value Proposition needs to add value and be realistic to what you can consistently deliver.

The Customer Value Proposition can be emotional, logical, or rational, or a combination. Benefits are what adds value for the customer. Be sure to verbally communicate these benefits to motivate the sale.

What to Bring to Your Sales Presentation

Now that we've reviewed some key concepts of meetings and presentations, let's have a look at some of the elements that you should have in a sales presentation to build a relationship. Having a face-to-face presentation (in-person or virtually) requires some visual elements.

These can be a combination of a visual presentation, marketing and information materials, samples, demonstrations and examples of success for others. Let's take some time to review how to prepare to turn our prospects into customers during a presentation.

The Visual Presentation

Providing information and delivering details of data, research and testimonials can all be included in your sales presentations. There are several options for presentation materials some of the most widely used are PowerPoint and Prezi.

While you can choose your presentation application, the components of your presentation, such as your slides need to be visible to the prospect and you should demonstrate ease of navigating.

When Presenting

Practice, Practice, Practice! Practicing will help ensure that you are comfortable with each presentation component and the technology that you will be using to present. The last thing that you want is for the focus to be on technology and distract from the information and communication process.

While the details around your meetings will dictate the type of presentation required, there are some standard visual presentation guidelines you may find helpful, especially if you are using something like PowerPoint and Prezi:

Cover Image: A strong cover image and opening slide. You want to attract the customer's attention. Also keep in mind this slide should be on the screen during introductions and will be viewed a longer time-than others. Make it count.

Data and key points: Statistics, graphs, charts, and data are all pieces of information that support your visual presentation and what you are communicating. The slides should not be full of words – that is your role. Communicating the key points of focus more thoroughly. Your customers do not want to be looking at slides full of words. Keep the slides simple with visual prompts.

References and Quotes: How your product has helped others makes it more relatable to the prospect, especially if it is the same industry. This is often referred to as social proof.

Customized content: Personalize your presentation for each meeting prospect. You have done the research on them, now use it. Customizing the presentation to grab their attention is the goal. You should try to align what you can with their industry data and company colours.

Next Steps Slide: The last slide of your presentation should be a direct call to action, communicating one or two next steps with the goal to gain the prospects commitment to action.

The Product

If you can demonstrate how the product works, do so. It is an opportunity for the customer to view, touch and use. Having a hands-on experience can motivate the customer. Ideally you want to show off your product or service. You want to showcase it at its best and demonstrate its benefits and customer value proposition.

Handouts

Having sales packs and information materials provides tangible information that the customer can reflect on after the meeting. This can be as simple as contact information or sales literature, or it can be something that's part of the presentation, such as a link or code directing them to download an app or demo on their phones while in the meeting. Determine the best way to minimize distractions and keep it simple since you want your meeting attendees to actively listen to you.

Your Team

Depending on the particulars of your business, you may have other people associated with your small business who could enhance the sales relationship. Preparation is key, whether you are working independently or as part of a team, it's important to prepare beforehand and ensure that everyone understands their role within the presentation. Ensure that the communication strategies, including the verbal and non-verbal elements are aligned and demonstrate a highly functioning team.

Confidence

You will want to demonstrate confidence in your presentation and your ability to deliver the message. The more you practice, the more confident you will become. Practice all components including timing, demonstrations and commitments. Verify everything needed for the presentation works. Do your best to make sure everything goes as planned and that your meetings and presentations meet and exceed your attendees' expectations.

Chapter Summary

In this chapter you have learned about preparing for meetings and presentations. You learned how to provide information about how your products or services can benefit a customer, and how to recognize appropriate meeting formats and platforms based on your customer's needs. You also learned about how you can generate buying motivation through strong communication in your meetings and presentations. You spent time learning the skills around meeting planning and preparation and worked through creating a meeting agenda and building a template to ensure all critical meeting preparation tasks are met. You spent time learning and the skills required to plan successful presentations. You is completed. You also learned about post meeting and presentation follow ups for building and sustaining your sales-based relationships and managing and maintaining the information you gather.

Regardless of your products or services, you are in the business of people, especially in the B2C sales environment. Your ability to nurture and grow client and business relationships through meetings, presentations and follow ups demonstrate a strong customer focused sales approach. It is now it is time to go and get those sales!

References

Adapted from Mehrabian A. Silent Messages: Implicit Communication of Emotions and Attitudes. 2nd ed. Belmont, California: Wadsworth Publishing Company; 1981. https://archive.org/details/silentmessagesim00mehr

What is Customer Experience (2019) Bordeaux, J. Hubspot Blog, retrieved from https://blog.hubspot.com/service/what-is-customer-experience, Erin Wilson, 2020

ABCs of Relationship Selling Through Service: Futrell & Valvasori, McGraw-Hill Ryerson; 6th edition (2015)

Making a Great First Impression. (n.d). Mind Tools. Retrieved from: https://www.mindtools.com/CommSkll/FirstImpressions.htm

10 Verbal Communication Skills Worth Mastering. (n.d). Smith, T. Little Things Matter. Retrieved from: https://www.littlethingsmatter.com/blog/2010/11/30/10-verbal-communication-skills-worth-mastering/

What is your Dominant Communication Style? https://www.keela.co/communications-style-quiz, Erin Wilson, 2021

http://www.strategicbusinessinsights.com/vals/presurvey.shtml

https://www.investopedia.com/terms/a/adaptive-selling.asp

Jerry Acuff and Wally Wood, The Relationship Edge in Business (Hoboken, NJ: John Wiley & Sons, Inc., 2006): 149–150

Geoffrey James, "How to Build Customer Relationships—An Interview with Jerry Acuff," Selling Power (March 2006): 43–46

Eileen McDargh, "Provide Great Service," Sales & Service Excellence 10 (June 2010): 10

John Werner, "Customer Complaints: A Gift in Disguise," ASQ Six Sigma Forum Magazine (May 2013): 28–30

Chia-Chi Chang, "When Service Fails: The Role of the Salesperson and the Customer," Psychology & Marketing 23 (March 2006): 203–224

Steil, L., Barker, L., & Watson, K. (n.d.). SIER hierarchy of active listening. Provenmodels, accessed August 1, 2011, http://www.provenmodels.com/554. (SIER model)

http://meetingsift.com/the-six-types-of-meetings/

http://meetingsift.com/how-to-run-successful-meetings/

Benson, Kierra. Top Online Meeting Software to Know by TechFunnel Contributors - Last Updated on May 25, 2021
https://www.techfunnel.com/information-technology/11-best-virtual-meeting-platforms-for-business/

Ty Collins, October 21, 2020 Top 14 online meeting platforms
https://calendly.com/blog/online-meeting-platforms/

https://www.pipedrive.com/en/blog/sales-presentation

www.ingramcontent.com/pod-product-compliance
Lightning Source LLC
Chambersburg PA
CBHW070254220526
45465CB00004B/1615